519

IMMEDIATELY AFTER THE TRIBULATION

- The Return of Jesus Christ
- The Resurrection of Saints
- The Rapture of the Church

By

Moreton. F. Scruby

Price $1.00

Send all orders

TO

JOHN J. SCRUBY PRINTING CO.
1409 East Fifth Street
Dayton 3, Ohio

CONTENTS

~~~~~~

*Give me the liberty to know, to utter,
and to argue freely according to conscience above all other liberties.*
                        — Milton.

*And What Is Writ Is Writ,
Would It Were Worthier.*
                        — Byron.

CHAPTER ONE

"In the Volume of the Book"

"For we have not followed cunningly devised fables, when we made known unto you the power and coming of our Lord Jesus Christ, but were eyewitnesses of His majesty. . . . We have also a more sure word of prophecy; whereunto ye do well that ye take heed, as unto a light that shineth in a dark place, until the day dawn, and the day star rise in your hearts." 2 Peter 1:16, 19.

The apostle Peter sets forth the fact of the second coming of Christ. In substance he says: I know Christ is coming back again. I am sure He is coming back to reign. It is certain because there is a sure proof of it. The sure proof is the word prophecies of the Scriptures. The clear, plain, straightforward statements of the fact.

Saying Is Believing

With Peter, saying was believing, if the Lord said it, and He did say it. We read our Lord's statement concerning His first advent in Hebrews 10:7: "Then said I, Lo, I come (in the volume of the book it is written of Me)". What He declares to be true regarding His first advent is just as vitally correct concerning His second coming. In the whole volume of the Bible it is stated that Christ will return. From the opening page, to the concluding page, it is found in chapter after chapter, and book following book. It would not be difficult to show in a detailed way, how the doctrine is presented in text and type, parable and hyperbole, in exalted song and rarest rhetoric, in noblest poetry and dramatic imagery, in extended passage and sententious statement, in simile and symbol.

The word prophecies of the Bible constitute the sure proof of Christ's return. So we can believe, with Peter, in the second coming of Christ because of the place of precedence and prominence given to it in both the Old and the New Testaments. Its importance is established by ample evidence. In all his epistles, Paul refers but thirteen times to baptism; while he writes of the Lord's return fifty times. One verse in every thirty in the New Testament speaks of Christ's second coming. It is well understood that the first advent is a prominent theme of the Old Testament, but it contains twenty times as many references to the second advent. In the New Testament alone Christ's second coming is mentioned three hundred and nineteen times. It is spoken of twenty-five times as often as the cross, and fifteen times as frequently as the resurrection.

Seeing Is Believing

"We have also a more sure word of prophecy" says Peter. Actually he is saying: The sure proof of Christ's return is made more sure. This is a lot of proof. The more sure proof is the picture prophecies of the Scriptures. Peter declares that when he preached the second coming of Christ, he did not reach into the Scriptures and pick out isolated and unrelated passages, forming them in a fable of fancy and fiction. Said he: I told you what I had actually seen with my own eyes. Seeing was believing with Peter, if he saw it, and he did. He declares he and James and John "were eyewitnesses of His majesty". That is, he asserts he saw the coming of the Lord in majesty. He had seen His coming in ignominy and had been associated intimately with Him as one of the twelve. Now he contends He had also witnessed His coming in majesty — or glory. The second coming would be as real as the first. His eyes could not deceive him. This takes us to the transfiguration event in the life of Jesus as recorded in Matthew 17:1-21. It is suggested "the transfiguration scene contains, in miniature, all the elements of the future kingdom in manifestation: 1) The Lord, not in humiliation, but in glory. 2) Moses, glorified, representative of the redeemed who have passed through death into the kingdom. 3) Elijah, glorified, representative of the redeemed who have entered into the kingdom by translation. 4) Peter, James, John, not glorified, representatives (for the moment) of Israel in the flesh in the future kingdom. 5) The multitude at the foot of the mountain, representative of the nations who are to be brought into the kingdom after it is established". Very vividly and dramatically, the transfiguration scene pictured the coming of the Lord in glory, and Peter saw it. This kind of proof is conclusive with the apostle. It would not be ignored by him. It could not be explained away. Christ is coming back again to earth.

CHAPTER TWO

"Surely I Come"

On one occasion Goethe wrote a statement to the effect that one of the greatest forces in the universe is an idea whose time has come. By this he meant to say that when, in the unfolding of events, the time comes for an idea, or a plan to materialize into actuality, no other force is strong enough to stop it from coming to pass. This may, or may not be true in the natural realm, but it is tremendously true in the spiritual. God has plans. He works them — and they work. God's purposes cannot be thwarted. The Almighty cannot be frustrated. What God proposes He accomplishes. His decrees are destined to materialize.

All Scripture is to be interpreted in the light of Scripture already fulfilled. Prophecy can be interpreted in the light of prophecy that has come to pass. History has a way of repeating itself. What has happened can happen again. Christ came once as the Lamb of God to be slain; He will return as the Lion of the Tribe of Judah to reign.

Coming Surely

He is coming surely! This is not a myth. It is not a mirage. It is not make-believe. It is not a Hollywood stunt. It is not fiction, but fact. There is no event in history more clearly established than the first advent of Christ. There is more evidence to prove that Jesus Christ once lived upon the earth than that George Washington was a general and the father of his country; or that Abraham Lincoln ever lived and was the emancipator of slaves.

Jesus did live. He did "go about doing good, and healing all that were oppressed of the devil", Acts 10: 38, opening the eyes of the blind, unstopping the ears of the deaf, cleansing the lepers, loosing the tongues of the dumb, delivering the demon-controlled, even raising the dead. But since all the prophecies concerning Christ were not fulfilled at His first coming it remains as a matter of reason that there must be another advent, or many of the prophecies will remain unfulfilled.

Yes, He is coming surely! We have the proclamation of the fact by Jesus Himself. Whatever else men may say, or think, about our Lord, surely no one will accuse Him of being a deceiver. It will also be admitted He must have known more than anyone else about His life and plans. We believe Him therefore, when in no uncertain terms He proclaims the fact of His second coming. We cannot misunderstand such language as Matthew 16: 27: "The Son of man *shall* come in the glory of His Father with His angels"; or the promise made in John 14: 3: *"I will* come again". Underscore the *"shall"* and the *"will"*.

As if to authenticate all He had said about His return during His earthly ministry and to give added weight to His words previously spoken, Jesus speaks from heaven, and closes the Bible with the significant statement: "He which testifieth these things saith, Surely I come". Revelation 22: 20. We have the proclamation by Jesus, and the attestation by the witnesses from heaven. In the first chapter of Acts we find a scene so sublime, so inspiring, so completely out of this world, that no human tongue, pen, or brush can adequately describe it. Christ has left His "ivory palaces" and has come into this "world of woe". He has lived, loved and labored among men. He has been "lifted up" on the

cross, and has laid down His life. He has left the tomb
in triumph. Now He is leading His disciples out to
the Mount of Olives. He is discussing events of interest
in His plan for the ages. Suddenly a "cloud" appears.
It is the bright light of the Shekinah. He is lifted up
to heaven before their very eyes. As they stand there
in wide-eyed, and open-mouthed amazement, held spell-
bound by this marvelous phenomenon, two angels in
glistening apparel stand by them, "which also said, Ye
men of Galilee, why stand ye gazing up into heaven?
this same Jesus, which is taken up from you into
heaven, shall so come in like manner as ye have seen
Him go into heaven". Acts 1: 11. Underscore the words
"shall so come".

He is coming surely! It is the only unfulfilled fact
in the life and ministry of Jesus as stated in the glorious
Gospel concerning Him. There are seven fundamental
facts concerning our Lord as set forth in Scripture.

The first fact is His supernatural birth. Luke 1: 35.
Jesus was conceived by the Holy Spirit, begotten of
God and born of the virgin.

The second fact is His sinless life. 2 Corinthians 5: 21.
The unbroken testimony of friend and foe alike from
the day of Christ's birth until this day is: "I find no
fault in this man". Luke 23: 4. God begot one perfect
Son, that He might bring all His sons to perfection.
God provided one sinless Saviour, that He might be
every sinner's Saviour.

The third fact concerning Christ is His substitution-
ary death. "He was wounded for our transgressions,
He was bruised for our iniquities". Isaiah 53: 5.

The fourth great fact is the sublime resurrection of
Christ. Luke 24: 39. Jesus came forth from the tomb
with a sublime, glorified body. It was not simply

the resurrection of influence, ideal, teaching, idea. It was a physical, triumphant resurrection.

The fifth fact is Christ's supreme exaltation. He ascended to heaven where He now sits at the right hand of God. "Who for the joy that was set before Him endured the cross, despising the shame, and is set down at the right hand of the throne of God." Hebrews 12:2.

The sixth fact is the sending forth of the Holy Spirit on the day of Pentecost according to promise. Acts 1:4. That was undoubtedly the greatest single event in all Christian history. It was the divine heat, the welding power of God, joining together hearts and lives into one great body, called the Church.

The final, and only unfulfilled fact in the life of Christ is His second coming. Each event is vital. All are essential. Lacking any of them we would have only a partial Gospel. To cut away any of them would be to mutilate the evangel. It is a matter of logic to conclude that if six of the events have already transpired — and they are historic facts — that the seventh will be just as literally fulfilled. Christ is coming surely! His return will be the vindication of His humiliation. It will give the right ending to the story.

> "Trusting in the literal word,
>   We look for Christ on earth again;
> Come, our everlasting Lord,
>   With all Thy saints to reign."

Coming Shortly

Christ is coming shortly! Guided by signs of the times, and on authority given by the Word of God, we believe that His coming is not a remote event. It will not be in the dim and distant future. Perhaps the words of Zephaniah 1:4, were never more true than

now, for we read: "The great day of the Lord is near,
it is near and hasteth greatly". That is to say, it is near
when certain signs are in evidence, and they surely
are today. Now, more than at any previous period, the
words of Paul in Romans 13:12 are applicable, for he
declares: "The night is far spent, the day is at hand".
At a time when society is plagued by industrial dis-
content and social unrest. When capital and labor are
looking at each other with blood in their eyes, and
rich and poor are at each other's throats. As great
social revolution comes resulting in the disintegration
of vast fortunes, and retribution for ill-gotten gains,
then it is that James envisions the coming of the Lord
and exhorts the oppressed laborer to: "Be patient . . .
unto the coming of the Lord. . . . Be ye . . . patient; stablish your hearts; for the coming of the Lord draweth
nigh". James 5:7, 8. Surely our hearts should vibrate
with hope and praise as we read the words of Hebrews
10:37: "For yet a little while, and He that shall come
will come, and will not tarry". Let our souls respond
in faithful anticipation and with fervent prayer —
"Amen. Even so, come, Lord Jesus". Revelation 22:20.

CHAPTER THREE

"Let no man deceive you"

Deception may be deadly and destructive, hence the warning, "Let no man deceive you by any means". 2 Thessalonians 2: 3. There is no realm where error and deception are as costly as in the sphere of Scripture truth. Bible doctrine is the steel in the Gospel structure. Error in doctrine constitutes a flaw in the steel that may weaken it and thus jeopardize the structure itself. Christians should be on their guard against error in teaching. Scripture doctrine is the blood in the body of Christian faith. Error is poison in the blood stream. It vitiates and victimizes the believer, robbing him of the fullness of spiritual strength and vital victory.

As a protest against the deadliness of deception in Bible doctrine, surely I will be indulged in some philosophical observations. I have in mind, specifically, error regarding the time of the return of Christ and the Rapture of the Church. As a warning to unwary souls Ovid averred: "Deadly poisons are often concealed under sweet honey". The easy bent of some souls toward gullibility caused Burton to beseech: "If the world will be gulled, let it be gulled". Machiavelli makes the remark: "Men are so simple and yield so much to necessity, that he who will deceive will always find him who will lend himself to be deceived". Mackenzie reminds us: "Mankind in the gross is a gaping monster, that loves to be deceived, and has seldom been disappointed". Balzac believed: "Men are such dupes by choice, that he who would impose upon others need never be at a loss to find ready victims". Knowing of some men's aversion to being convinced, and of their hesitancy to be corrected and to renounce the same in favor of truth, Nathaniel Cotton contends: "Yet we still hug to dear deceit". Mme. Sophie Arnould adds: "It is not being deceived, but undeceived, that renders us miserable". The strange readiness to be deceived led Terence to testify: "There is a demand in these days for men who can make wrong appear right". The practice of propagating religious error for advantage, caused Cowper to comment: "Stamps God's own name upon a lie just made, to turn a penny in the way of trade". The plain fact that anything said, or done, with the deliberate intent to deceive is deception, Dr. Johnson states: "Don't tell me of deception; a lie is a lie, whether it be a lie to the eye or a lie to the ear".

There is tragedy in being deceived. This is doubly true when the deceived has deceived because he was deceived. There are tears in knowing that one has been taught error by a tutor who sincerely believed he was teaching truth. For the most part, the people of God are trusting souls. They feel they have every right to believe what they are taught by those who are either self-appointed, or otherwise authorized to instruct. Wrote Bulwer-Lytton: "Of all the agonies in life, that which is most poignant and harrowing — that which for the time annihilates reason, and leaves our whole organization one lacerated, mangled heart — is the conviction that we have been deceived where we placed all the trust of love". What a tremendous responsibility rests upon the preacher of the Word of God!

A prayer: Lord, help Thy servants to faithfully and carefully and prayerfully discharge this obligation. O, Holy Spirit, "guide [them] into all truth" that they in turn may properly instruct others. Amen!

Christ is coming again surely. He will return shortly. So then, anything relating to His second advent is very vital. We should overlook nothing connected with this event. We need a clear understanding of the fact of His coming. A thorough knowledge of events leading to His return is desirable. To possess a working knowledge of Christ's coming and related doctrines is in order. It seems to me that here, especially, it is essential that we have a firm grasp of the truth. We cannot afford to be in error. If the coming of the Lord is as near as some are led to believe it to be, then proper and adequate preparation should be made by us for the glorious event. Let no one be deceived at any point regarding this vital matter.

The second coming, among other things, should be the theme of our teaching. It ought to be the topic of conversation among Christians. As the previous age drew to a close the faithful of the Lord looked forward to the first advent, and encouraged one another in their patient anticipation. The prophet tells us: "Then they that feared the Lord spake often one to another: and the Lord hearkened, and heard it, and a book of remembrance was written before Him for them that feared the Lord". Malachi 3:16. Surely they "spake often" to each other of His soon coming. This age draws to a close. Just as faithfully and fervently should we be "exhorting one another: and so much the more, as ye see the day approaching". Hebrews 10:25.

Satan and The Second Coming

So very vital is the truth of Christ's second coming that Satan is doing all he can to discount and discredit it. Jesus went out of His way to warn us that this would happen. The devil works hard to discount this

teaching by causing people to ignore it entirely, or to
show only slight interest in it. And the name of such
is "legion". This is tragic. However, knowing that
many are very much interested in the return of Christ,
and realizing that a great number believe it thoroughly,
Satan attempts to discredit the truth by deception and
delusion. Nothing delights the enemy more than to
plunge those who believe in Christ's return deep into
error if he can. We should be on our guard against
false teaching.

Jesus one day mounted His Olivetic pulpit and
preached a sermon in which He bridged the period
between His day and our day. He bridged the gap
between the beginning of the age and the end of the
age. He spoke eloquently of His return. In the sermon
He was very careful to warn us that there would be
many deceivers and great deceptions. By them many
would be deceived about His coming. Said He: "Take
heed that no man deceive you. For many shall come
in My name, . . . and shall deceive many. . . . And
many false prophets shall rise, and shall deceive many.
. . . For there shall arise false Christs, and false prophets, . . . if it were possible, they shall deceive the very
elect". Matthew 24: 4, 5, 11, 24. This did happen. So
much so, that Paul was led to repeat the warning
to believers of his day, and of all this age: "Let no
man deceive you by any means" about Christ's coming
and related events. 2 Thessalonians 2: 3. The tragedy
of tragedies is, that the warning has gone unheeded
by many in our day, and multitudes of earnest believers
in Christ's personal and pre-millennial coming have
been deceived by a false and deadly teaching. This
teaching is popular, widespread, harmful and *above
all unscriptural*. It misinterprets, and misapplies Scripture. Bible truth, Christian experience and a funda-

mental and vital principle of life are violated by it. It is an error of errors. It seriously wounds the blessed and beloved truth of Christ's second coming. *I refer to the widely taught and almost universally accepted teaching of the rapture of the Church before, or during, the coming Great Tribulation.* Yes, Christ will return for His Church. My heart — as perhaps does yours — thrills at the blessed prospect. To expect His coming, however, at any time before the end of the Great Tribulation, and the consummation of the age, is totally unwarranted from the standpoint of Scripture teaching.

CHAPTER FOUR

"The Unity of the Faith"

Now the purpose of this book is out! Now, perhaps, my theological head will soon roll. Or, will it? I pray it will not. I would not want to be guilty of misjudging my beloved brethren. Maybe they will "agree to differ, but resolve to love". This is my fervent hope. I desire to help, not to hinder. "Here I stand. I cannot do otherwise. God help me." (I will be permitted to quote Luther; even though I lack his courage, conviction and consecration.) I have been encouraged to hope that those who read this book will be charitable in their attitude because of something I read recently. The book dealt with the general subject of prophecy. The author did "earnestly contend for the faith which was once delivered unto the saints". Jude 3. It was a delight to read the clear Bible exposition. The second coming of Christ was beautifully and faithfully set forth. What an inspiration it was to read the author's able and impassioned plea for unity among believers. How my heart was thrilled with the warm words written regarding fellowship with the saints — "fellowship with saints, not on the ground of light, but life in Christ". Well, let me quote at length, then you will understand why I greatly appreciate these beautiful words and the noble sentiment.

"How much this is needed today! The Church of God is rent in pieces. Bickerings and quarrelings persist. And what is most galling is the fact that all saved by grace stand for the fundamentals of the faith. We agree on the essentials, yet we find time to separate and disagree on the non-essentials. Shame on us! We have brought dishonor upon our precious Saviour, and grieved the blessed Holy Spirit of God.

"Is there a remedy? There is. Let us get back to Bible teaching. A basic principle in Scripture is that we fellowship with saints not on the ground of light, but life in Christ. Everyone is redeemed by precious blood. Everyone is quickened by the Holy Spirit. Everyone is a member of the body of Christ. Everyone is destined to dwell with Christ throughout eternity. Now, some saints are weak in the faith. Others are hidebound denominationalists. Few are strong enough to enjoy Christian liberty. Most saints have to bear with me. Shall I then, not bear with them? 'Behold, how good and how pleasant it is for brethren to dwell together in unity!' ". Psalm 133:1.

I ask you: Isn't that delightful, and inspiring? It makes me proud to be known as a brother Believer, and also a brother Britisher! With such a plea before me, I can now proceed with the task at hand, and be sure all will be well with me. I need not fear excommunication. No one will call for my head. (I don't know why it is that a certain incident persists in coming to mind. I once heard the godly John McNeil preach. He was telling of something that he very much wanted to see happen. Then in an aside the "canny Scotsman" said: "But, I ha' me doots".)

Such pleas for unity often present a problem to me. In fact they sometimes leave me cold. I am asked to preserve "the unity of the Spirit", and to do so by accepting all that such brethren teach, whether it be true or false. Very often, with the pleader, "unity of the Spirit" means "unity of the faith". I am expected to agree with the things taught or else be considered a heretic, and as such be ostracised, or at least discriminated against. Yet Paul recognized the fact that at present, with our limited understanding, and diversified intellects, it is hardly possible for us all to think alike. When everyone thinks alike, then no one thinks at all, except the one who outlined the formula of faith and crammed it into the minds of all the others. Said Paul: "Endeavoring to keep the unity of the Spirit. . . . Till we all come in the unity of the faith". Ephesians 4: 3, 13. It is not our work to "think" out truth, but to "search the Scriptures"; not to determine, or to formulate factual truth but to receive it and to propagate it. With all too many of us, truth is what *we* believe; and error is what someone else holds if it does not agree with *our* views. Pilate had heard many views expressed about the same things, by different "authorities"; no wonder he asked: "What is truth?". John 18: 38. The "truth" to an atheist is the non-existence of a personal God. To the believer "truth", as it relates to Christian doctrine, is whatever is set forth as fact in the Scriptures. All kingdom, or gospel "truth" has been revealed in the Bible. There are to be no new or other revelations, only a clearer comprehension of what has been written. Peter assures us: "No prophecy of the Scripture is of any private interpretation. For the prophecy came not in old time by the will of man: but holy men of God spake as they were moved by the Holy Ghost". 2 Peter 1: 20, 21. No man is infallible. Any of us may be wrong when interpreting Scripture. We are but human. Only God the Holy Spirit can accurately interpret the Word. Surely it is vital that we do not "add to", "take from", or "wrest" the Scriptures. Only Scripture is completely correct. Hence Christ declares: "The Spirit of truth . . . will guide you into all truth". John 16: 13.

CHAPTER FIVE

"Believe it Not"

In the case we are considering, the preacher proceeds to present a view of Christ's coming that must be considered unsound because it is unscriptural. Here is one of the numerous statements made in the book referred to in which the author propagates a false view of the second advent: "This leads us to a consideration of the order of events at the coming. But, before we proceed, let us get a clear, Scriptural conception of the 'second advent'. It is but one event in two stages. And in this it may be likened to the first coming of Christ. He came first to Bethlehem, and then thirty-three years later to Jerusalem. So He shall come first of all into the air for His saints (1 Thessalonians 4:16, 17), and some years later return with them to initiate His world wide kingdom (Revelation 20:4)".

We are asked to accept this as being truth when it is dangerous error. In the first place there is no Scripture that gives any ground for saying that the second coming will be "one event in two stages". This is a human invention. If Christ coming to Bethlehem was one coming and His coming "thirty-three years later to Jerusalem" was another coming, then this gives us two comings and not one. If this be true, then every time Jesus came to any place during His earthly life and ministry should be considered as a "coming", and the total number of such "comings" would be considerable. If there were many "comings" then let us cease to talk about the "first coming" as though there was but one. If what we are told here is correct, then the first coming was followed by a second and a third and a fourth — and so on, ad infinitum; and I might say ad nauseam. Likewise, the second coming, when it takes place, will be followed by a third coming — and then other comings.

I know of no statement in the Scriptures telling of a third coming. But I do recall a statement in Hebrews 9: 28: "And unto them that look for Him shall He appear *the second time* without sin unto salvation". Christ did say: "I will come again", but never did He even infer that He would come again, and again. Why should we be asked to believe something that is not taught in the Bible? If it were, it would be absurd to talk about a first and second coming, limiting the number to but two.

Then again, while the statement is made in the foregoing quotation that "He shall come first of all into the air for His saints (1 Thessalonians 4: 16, 17), and some years later return with them", yet not one word of proof is or could be given, because there is no Bible proof. Would it be unreasonable to ask for proof? Is it too much to say that assertion is not proof? Let me give you the exact quotation, to which the writer refers, as we have it in the Bible. Then answer my question as to whether anything is said, or even intimated, that warrants anyone stating that "some years will elapse between Christ's coming *for* His saints in the air, and then return *with* Him to initiate His world-wide kingdom". Here is the Bible statement; read it carefully: "For the Lord Himself shall descend from heaven with a shout, and with the voice of the archangel, and with the trump of God: and the dead in Christ shall rise first; then we which are alive and remain shall be caught up together with them in the clouds, to meet the Lord in the air; and so shall we ever be with the Lord".

Yes, "the Lord Himself shall descend . . . the dead in Christ shall rise" and "we which are alive and remain, shall be caught up together with them in the clouds". What for? "To meet the Lord in the air." Why? Well, I should say to greet Him and to return with Him, "and so shall we ever be with the Lord" where He will be. And where is that? On earth, reigning over His kingdom. Revelation 5:10. With this explanation in mind, consider the following. The book I referred to was read during a recent six-month Bible conference tour of Florida. Some days later I returned to my home in Dayton by airplane. Before I "took off", I sent a message to my wife stating I was returning and telling of the time of my coming "in the clouds". When I arrived my entire family were at the airport to "meet me". What happened? Did we all return to Florida where I had been for some weeks to "come some years later", or at a later time, to my home? You know we did not! They met me, and welcomed me, and we remained in Dayton, where we reside. Now why make the words of the Bible mean anything more, or other, than what they were intended to mean? The author advises "us to get a clear, Scriptural conception of the second advent". I should say concerning this view, that it is clearly unscriptural, and consequently confused and hazy. Let us take nothing for granted, and read nothing into the Bible account, but be content with what God has put there.

No Secret Coming

What I have written should help to point up the reason for Christ's urgent and repeated warning against being deceived regarding His coming. It seems that neither piety, nor sincerity, nor capability, nor all combined, make one immune from the possibility of being deceived. For Jesus stresses the fact that "the very elect" may be led into error. It is significant that the warning is coupled with the positive preaching of Jesus in which He states there will be no "secret coming". He must have anticipated this false teaching, for He declares: "Then if any shall say unto you, Lo, here is Christ, or there; believe it not. . . . wherefore if they shall say unto you, Behold, He is in the desert; go not forth: behold, He is in the secret chambers; believe it not". Matthew 24: 23, 26. I am inclined to do as Jesus suggested — "Believe it not". When I hear, or read of the "secret coming", or the "secret rapture" there leaps into my mind the positive assertion of the Master in the words following those just recorded: "For as the lightning cometh out of the East, and shineth even unto the West; so shall also the coming of the Son of Man be". Matthew 24: 26. There is no secret about the flash of lightning that splits the sky and races across the heavens. How could a strange and spectacular scene such as the catching away of multitudes of people from the earth with no visible vehicle of conveyance; accompanied by the shout of Christ, and the voice of the archangel and the trumpet of God; the opening of the graves across the earth; together with astronomical phenomena filling the heavens and the descent of Christ with myriads of angels through the sky, be kept secret? It requires too much imagination to believe this. More than I have. But, if the Bible taught such a thing I would believe it very readily, because I know God could and would cause it to make sense. God does nothing in secret. God operates openly. An "iron curtain" is a device of evil men. God has nothing to hide. Thus when Jesus states in

Luke 21: 27: "And then shall they see the Son of man coming in a cloud with power and great glory"; and when John also declares in Revelation 1: 7: "Behold, He cometh with clouds and every eye shall see Him", these words become representative of all Scripture teaching regarding His coming.

I am quite sure that a casual, or even a careful, searching of Scripture would not bring forth any statement telling of a "secret coming", or a "secret rapture". This is not open to debate. It is settled by the Word of God — which is the final word, from which there can be no appeal. No word can be found to support the contention that He will come *for* His saints, and then again, at a later date, *with* them. Proper interpretation of Scripture entirely rules out the theory of a coming before, or even during the Great Tribulation. *"Immediately after the tribulation of those days . . . shall appear the sign of the Son of man in heaven: and then shall all the tribes of the earth mourn, and they shall see the Son of man coming in the clouds of heaven with power and great glory. And He shall send His angels with a great sound of a trumpet, and they shall gather together His elect from the four winds, from one end of heaven to the other."* Matthew 24: 29-31. The particular point to be observed is *"Immediately after the tribulation"*.

Goethe says: "We are not deceived, we deceive ourselves". Meaning that if we refuse to consider proof, weigh evidence and accept facts when available, then ignorance, or error is deliberate and we shall be held accountable. So much has been written in the Scriptures concerning the fact and the manner of Christ's return that there is no good reason for doubting or being deceived. James says: "Be ye doers of the word and not hearers only, deceiving your own selves". James 1: 22.

We need a new conception of right and wrong to save us from the deadliness of evil and error. How can we know the truth? Not by taking it out of the air — but by a careful, prayerful study of the Scriptures. Not by listening to men expound—but by letting the Spirit reveal the truth to us. "If any man will do His will, He shall know of the doctrine, whether it be of God." John 7:17.

CHAPTER SIX
The Return and the Rapture
"Immediately after the tribulation"

Now we plunge into the effort of showing that it is a bad blunder on the part of anyone to suppose that the coming of Christ and the Rapture of the Church will be at any time before the very last day of this present dispensation. It is quite certain that the Bible does not teach an "any-moment" coming of Christ *"for His saints"* to return at some time later *"with His saints"*. There can be no resurrection or rapture of saints until the end of the age. There will be a *second coming and no subsequent advents.*

I am writing these words in 1950. In 1912 I began an intensive and extensive study of the Scriptures. At no time have I found even so much as a single syllable in the Scriptures which states that there will be a "secret coming" at "any-moment" and that Christ will come *"for His saints"* and following an interval of months, or years, *"with His saints"*. Is this a startling statement? Is it heresy? Then let me quote some words written a number of years ago by Thomas M. Chalmers in the *Jewish Missionary Magazine*. Dr. Chalmers was a scholar, but nonetheless a saint. Said he: "We have never been able to accept a rapture before the great tribulation because it is not in the Word. Fifty readings of the Greek New Testament never showed us a single verse in which it is taught". I think the fact this learned man had read the New Testament fifty times in the original language should make him something of an authority. If I had read it fewer times in the English language, and not at all in the Greek, I would hesitate to controvert his statement about the Scriptures. Surely his words carry weight because of his thorough and frequent readings of the New Testament in the Greek.

The battle-cry of orthodoxy is: "Back to the Bible". Well and good — then we will go to the Bible and see what it actually teaches about the time of the coming. "The entrance of Thy word giveth light." Psalm 119: 130. Dr. Charles Hodge asserts: "The only legitimate method of controverting a doctrine which purports to be founded on the Scriptures is the exegetical". Meaning, of course, that the way to combat error is to preach Bible truth. Truth is not what men say, but what God states in the Bible. I ask only that we consider exactly what the Bible says, and nothing else.

Dr. Samuel Henry Kellogg, who, out of a long and varied life has been described as: "one of the foremost theologians, scholars, missionaries, pastors, preachers and philologists of his time", once wrote: "There shall certainly be *one* return of Christ to this world, and that the presentation of the completed Church before Him is to take place in connection with that one future return".

Pre- and Post-Tribulation-Rapturism

The Bible states "We . . . shall be caught up together with them in the clouds, to meet the Lord in the air". 1 Thessalonians 4: 17. This catching away of the Church from the earth "to meet the Lord in the air" is called "The Rapture". Mind you, the word "Rapture" is not used in the Bible. However, the thought it expresses of being "caught up" is definitely Scriptural. Pre, as you may know, means before. Post, as is well known, means after. It is properly understood from such direct statements as Daniel 12: 1, and Matthew 24: 21, that this present age will close with a period of unprecedented and universal trouble called "The Great Tribulation". The language is very clear. Daniel declares: "And there shall be a time of trouble, such as never was since there was a nation, even to that same time". The words of Christ are even more explicit and expressive: "For there shall be great tribulation, such as was not since the beginning of the world to this time, no, nor ever shall be [again]".

During recent years it has been generally taught that the Church will be raptured, or "caught up to meet the Lord" before the Tribulation, and thus will be absent during this time of trouble. This we will call *Pre-tribulation-rapturism*. In so far as the Church Fathers and the Bible expositors through the centuries, until recent years, have had anything to say about the subject, they have taught that the Church will remain on the earth throughout the entire age, going through the Tribulation, thus facing the Antichrist and unchristian and antichristian forces to the end of the age and then will be Raptured. This we will call *"Post-tribulation-rapturism"*.

Let us keep the definitions in mind: Pre- and Post-tribulation-rapturism. Pre-tribulation-rapturism: Rapture of the Church before the Tribulation. Post-tribulation-rapturism: Rapture of the Church following the Tribulation.

A Modern "Ism"

Post-tribulation-rapturism is as old as Scripture. Pre-tribulation-rapturism is a modern "ism". Until the year 1830 all teaching of the Church was of Post-tribulation variety. The Pre-tribulation teaching was born early in the nineteenth century. Quite evidently it was an illegitimate birth. It was sired by Satan. The circumstances that gave it birth prove this. A woman, named Margaret Macdonald, who was associated with a religious group in Great Britain known as the "Irvingites", mothered the illegitimate fallacy. Irving-ism meetings featured so-called "Spirit manifestations", "speaking with other tongues", and "giving messages in the Spirit". The Irvingite woman, in such a meeting, and while supposedly "under the power" of the Holy Spirit, was given a message which was believed by her to be from the Lord. She claimed the Lord re-vealed to her that Old and New Testament writers, the early Church Fathers and subsequent saints — anyone, and everyone who ever contended for Post-tribulation-rapturism — all were wrong. He revealed to her — so she believed — that the Church would be raptured before and not "immediately after the tribu-lation". The teaching took root for the first time when men like Irving, who headed this sect, took the new revelation, and built it into a doctrine that has be-come almost universally accepted by adventists. It seemed to count for nothing that this new revelation was in direct contradiction to all teaching of the Bible on the subject and that it nullified all that had been taught about it by the faithful Church for eighteen centuries.

Proof of the Foregoing

Assertion is not proof. Contention calls for authen-tication. Proof of the origin of Pre-tribulation-raptur-ism is available. I present this documented evidence. It is authentic. It is conclusive. "On May 1, 1861, seventy-seven years ago, (written January 1938) there was published in England a book by 'R. N.', which initials were those of Dr. R. Nolan, an M. D., who was an enthusiastic member of the Irvingite Church. The title of the book was "The Restoration of Apostles and

Prophets in the Catholic Apostolic Church", which was
the name adopted by Edward Irving's organization.
This book has long been out of print, but through the
courtesy and kindness of Rev. J. A. Anderson of Aber-
deen, Scotland, I have been privileged to read a copy
of Dr. Nolan's book. In it is this tremendously important statement by Dr. Nolan, a portion of which
I have put in capital letters for proper emphasis: "Marvelous light was shed upon Scripture and especially
on the doctrine of the second advent by the revived
spirit of prophecy. In the following account by Miss
M. M. .... [Margaret Macdonald], of an evening during which the power of the Holy Ghost rested upon her
for several successive hours in mingled prophecy and
vision, we have an instance: FOR WE FIRST SEE THE
DISTINCTION BETWEEN THAT FINAL STAGE OF
THE LORD'S COMING, WHEN EVERY EYE SHALL
SEE HIM, AND HIS PRIOR APPEARING IN GLORY
TO THEM THAT LOOK FOR HIM . . . SHE [Miss
M. M. ....] WRITES: 'I FELT THIS NEEDED TO BE
REVEALED, AND THAT THERE WAS A GREAT
DARKNESS AND ERROR ABOUT IT; but suddenly
what it was burst upon me with glorious light' ".

Typical Teaching Of The Church Fathers

I have said, "Until the year 1830 all teaching of the
Church was of the Post-tribulation variety". I take
my own medicine and admit that "assertion is not
proof". It is not possible here to give numerous and
extensive quotations. Let me suggest to those who are
interested enough to do so, that this assertion can be
verified by consulting books written by Church Fathers. Books on religious themes by authors of early
or modern times are to be found in most public libra-
ries. To point up what you would find, I quote from

Irenæus who wrote before the year 202: "It is manifest therefore, that of these potentates, he who is to come [meaning the Antichrist] shall slay three, and subject the remainder to his power. . . . And they [the ten kings] shall lay [Woman] Babylon waste, and burn her ' with fire, and shall give their kingdom to the beast, *and put the Church to flight.* . . . It is said, 'There shall be tribulation such as has not been since the beginning, neither be [again]'. *For this is the last contest of the righteous [the Church] in which, when they overcome,* they are crowned with incorruption. . . . All these and other words are spoken in reference to the resurrection of the just, *which takes place after the coming of Antichrist*".

Hippolytus was a contemporary of Irenæus. In his writings appear these statements: "Concerning the tribulation of the persecution [the persecution to be experienced during the tribulation] *which is to fall upon the Church* from the adversary [the Antichrist]. . . . That refers to the one thousand two hundred and threescore days during which the tyrant [the Antichrist] is to reign *and persecute the Church.* . . . Then Antichrist will appear. . . . *When he makes war against the saints, and persecutes them, then may we [Christians] expect the manifestation of the Lord from heaven*".

Ponder these passages. They are typical of the teaching of the Church Fathers from the days of the Apostles until the regretable birth of Pre-tribulation-rapturism by Margaret Macdonald in 1830. Not one author, or teacher consulted in a long list, even so much as hints at a rapture of the Church, or Christians, before the Great Tribulation, until the "ism" began in the 19th century. A theologian like Augustine wrote while commenting on Daniel 7:25: "He who reads this passage, even half-asleep, cannot fail to see that the kingdom of Antichrist shall fiercely, though for a short time, assail the Church".

"Try the Spirits"

There is a genuine work of the Holy Spirit, including "Spirit manifestations," etc., but there is also the counterfeit. This experience of Margaret Macdonald's falls into that category. Jesus taught in John 16: 13, 14: "Howbeit when He, the Spirit of truth, is come, He will guide you into all truth: . . . whatsoever He shall hear, that shall He speak: and He will show you things to come. . . . for He shall receive of Mine, and shall show it unto you". This allegedly "Spirit" taught woman was shown "things [allegedly] to come" but they were directly opposed to the "things" called "Mine". Therefore, and I say this guardedly, this "Spirit" revelation was given by a demon spirit, and not the Holy Spirit. No wonder John was inspired to add later, by way of serious admonition: "Beloved, believe not every spirit, but try the spirits whether they are of God: because many false prophets have gone out into the world". 1 John 4: 1. How striking these words are. A false revelation, given by a spurious spirit, to a deluded woman, has turned a great army of sincere and godly men and women into "false prophets". Thus, "many false prophets have gone out into the world" and are unwittingly being led to "deceive many", "in the latter times . . . giving heed to seducing spirits, and doctrines of devils". Matthew 24: 11; 1 Timothy 4: 1. I realize this is a serious charge to make, and it is not made lightly. There are tears in it. Of nothing am I more sure than that the overwhelming majority of Christian teachers and preachers are sincerely desirous of, and prayerfully attempting to prop-

agate truth, all the truth, and only the truth. With
many, teaching the error of Pre-tribulation-rapturism
is not a deliberate design to deceive — it is the tragic
result of themselves being mistaught. More and more
we realize what a tremendous responsibility it is to
"preach the Word". May God grant us to "know
the truth" and faithfully preach it! Amen!

A Friendly But Frank Discussion

For many years I have felt an urge to publish a
treatise on the fallacy of Pre-tribulation-rapturism. Day
and night it has been upon my heart. Many, many
people have encouraged me to do so. Until now I have
curbed the urge. I have refrained for one reason especially. I wanted such a thesis to be written so as
to embarrass no one. It must be presented in a friendly
fashion, and yet should be frankly discussed. I resolved
not to write until, or unless, I could do so without
referring in any way to the popular teaching of the
Rapture before the Tribulation. Could I present the
Post-tribulation-rapture teaching as though a contrary
view did not exist? If so, then, and only then, would
I make the attempt. I know now that such an undertaking is practically an impossibility. The only justi-
fiable reason for such a book would be to show the
utter fallacy of the common and contrary teaching. The
only way of showing how Scriptural and reasonable
Post-tribulation-rapturism is, would be to reveal how
unscriptural and unreasonable Pre-tribulation-rapturism is.

An attempt to show that the Church will be Raptured following the Tribulation would be unnecessary
if the work was to come into the hands only of those
untaught in the error of Pre-tribulation-rapturism.
It could be of interest and value especially only to

those who had been instructed in the false view, for the purpose would be to undo what had been done, and to present the truth with the hope that it might be accepted and error repudiated.

My hesitation stemmed from my desire to "keep the unity of the Spirit in the bond of peace". I have refrained from making my ministry divisive. I have wanted to cross swords with no one. I am fully aware of, and greatly appreciate, the piety, sincerity and the ability of my brethren in and out of the ministry. The fact that many hold to the Pre-tribulation-rapture view in no way reflects upon the godliness and earnestness of most. The most sincere and capable of us may be mistaken, and in a case like this, the mistake is tragic because of the harm that may be caused by hindering proper preparation for the coming of the Lord. The error is detrimental, even deadly, because there is the danger it will deter the development of sufficient faith to enable many to endure who might find themselves plunged into the Tribulation which they expected to escape by being removed from the earth by means of the Rapture before the fury of it commenced. It might be well to remember the words of Christ in Matthew 24:13: "But he that shall *endure unto the end,* the same shall be saved". It is quite clear that *"the end"* referred to is "the end of the age" and, therefore the end of the Great Tribulation.

CHAPTER SEVEN
"Search the Scriptures"

I suggest, as we plunge into the attempt to discover exactly what the Scriptures teach about the time of the Church's Rapture, we agree to emulate the example of the Berean Brethren as Paul tells it in Acts 17:11: "They received the word with all readiness of mind, and searched the Scriptures daily, whether these things were so". I have no doubt about what would happen if we "searched the Scriptures" and accepted the clear, plain, straight-forward statements found therein. Let Scripture speak for itself. It would be well for us to agree not to attempt any fanciful or forced interpretations.

"More of Us Wrong"

During my pastorate I taught Bible doctrine in a Bible Institute for three terms. Quite frequently I would say something like this to the students: "Now this is what I believe the Bible teaches about the subject in hand. However, I may be wrong because I am but human. I urge you not to park your brains with me, but keep them and allow the Holy Spirit to instruct your mind. Let your convictions be prompted by God and not provided by man. I advise this, because if I am wrong and you agree with my teaching, then you too, will be wrong. That will make a lot more of us wrong".

No Support For Pre-Tribulation-Rapturism

Frequently something like this has happened. I was conducting a Bible conference in Boone, Iowa. The pastor invited me to his home one evening for dinner. During the meal he remarked to me: "Mr. Scruby, you may be interested in an experience I had recently. The men of my church asked me to teach the Book of Revelation in our Sunday School class. I consented to do so, with the understanding they would agree to study it without helps, such as books, or commentaries. They promised to study it as though it were a new book to them. I confess I knew little about the book except what I had learned in Bible School. As I read and studied The Revelation I was surprised to find that nothing in it, so far as I could see, supported the teaching I had received concerning the Rapture of the Church before the Tribulation. Everything contradicted the teaching. The further I went the clearer it became, to me, that the Church would be present on earth during the days of the Tribulation". He did not know what my position was and was quite delighted to learn that I agreed with him, so did not consider him a heretic.

"The Church on Earth During the Tribulation"

During the past summer, while speaking daily in a missionary and Bible convention, at the close of a service, the minister directing the service said to me before I left the platform: "You may remember some conversations we had together several years ago about the Church and the Rapture. I was inclined to agree with you then, and the more I have studied the Scriptures since, the more I have been convinced the Church will be on earth during the Tribulation".

"Somewhat Confused"

Recently I had an experience that pointed up the presumption of many people today regarding the time

of the Rapture. I was delivering a series of addresses
on Bible prophecy in a certain city under the auspices
of a group called the "Christian Layman's Prophetic
Testimony". At the close of one of the services a
group gathered about me. In the group were some of
the officials of the organization. Acting as spokesman
for them, one person said: "We are somewhat confused.
Other speakers whom we have had emphasized the
point that many of the things spoken of by you will
occur following the Rapture of the Church. You have
not said anything that would indicate you believe this.
In fact we gather from your messages you may believe
the opposite. What *do* you believe?". To this I replied:
"You have asked me a point-blank question, I will
give you an answer just as direct. I do not believe
the Church will be raptured before the Tribulation
because I believe this teaching to be unscriptural".
Then the questions came "thick and fast".

The chairman of the "Testimony" said: "We supposed that the Rapture of the Church before the Tribulation was taught and believed by everyone". To this
I replied: "I notice you are advertising Dr. So-and-So
as your next Conference speaker. I also see from the
notices that one of the addresses announced is, 'Will
Believers Go Through the Tribulation?'. Believing his
answer to that question will no doubt be in the affirma-
tive, I am greatly surprised that he has announced the
theme". "Oh", said the chairman, "He didn't announce
it. He sent us a long list of subjects and told us to
pick from it the ones we would be interested in. We
picked this one". I asked: "Do you have any idea what
he will say, if he uses that sermon subject?". "No",
was the reply. "Then you may be in for the surprise
of your life, because I think I know what the speaker
will have to say, and it won't be Pre-tribulation-raptur-

ism. If anything, it will be Post-tribulation-rapturism".
Needless to say that confounded the group and raised
more questions.

A Noted Preacher's Post-Tribulation Views

The advertising for the coming conference described
the speaker as "So-and-So, D.D., Litt.D., L.L.D., F.R.
G.S., of ...., Canada. World Famous Missionary
Leader and Bible Expositor. One of the Ablest Ex-
ponents of Prophetic Truth of our Day". You may be
interested in what this truly noted and equally sincere
and godly preacher has written about the subject. Well,
here it is, in part: "And now, after years of study and
prayer, I am absolutely convinced there will be no
Rapture *before* the Tribulation, but that the Church
will undoubtedly be called upon to face the Antichrist,
and that Christ will come at the close and not at the
beginning of that awful period. I believed the other
theory simply because I was taught it, but when I
began to search the Scriptures for myself, whether
these things were so, I discovered that there is not a
single verse in the Bible that upholds the pre-tribulation theory, but that the uniform teaching of the Word
of God is for a post-tribulation rapture. Pre-millennial,
always, everywhere pre-millennial, but post-tribulation".

CHAPTER EIGHT
Saints and Scholars Take Issue

I refrained from stating the name of the man of God referred to in the previous chapter because he still lives. However, there is no reason for not giving the name of Edmund Shackleton, and quoting, in part, what he has written in his book, "Will the Church Escape the Great Tribulation?".

"Fascinating" but "False"

"There is something about this theory apart from its promise of deliverance from the persecution under the Antichrist, which renders it very fascinating. My own mind was under its spell for about five years. It was not without a struggle that I was induced to admit the possibility of it being false, and to set myself to examine its alleged Scriptural foundation. Having first prayed to God to take away my strong bias for the doctrine, if it were untrue, I tested, to the best of my ability, by Scripture, all the arguments which I have heard advanced in its support. I found to my surprise that the arguments for it were of the most unsatisfactory character; in fact, that almost any doctrine, no matter how erroneous, might be advocated on the same kind of hypothetical grounds. I have felt for some time a growing burden of regret that this ingenious figment of the human fancy should have been foisted upon God's people as if a most valuable truth."

"Religion of Sentiment"

Dr. S. P. Tregelles has written: "It is very manifest that the doctrine of a Second Coming of Christ, and

a secret Removal of the Church to be with Him, is
peculiarly suited to those who cherish the religion of
sentiment. . . . Are we to seek to be guided by other
hopes than those which animated the Apostolic Church?
They knew that days of darkness would set in before
Christ's coming; they were instructed respecting the
many Antichrists, and the final Antichrist, but so far
from their hope of the coming of the Lord and resurrection being thus set aside, they were able to look
forward through the darkness to the brightness of the
morning".

"No Proof In the Bible"

A Chinese medical missionary, the Rev. John A.
Anderson, in his book entitled: "The Church, the Chart
and the Coming" has this interesting observation to
make: "The truths which the following pages are
written to elucidate are surprisingly solemn, yet tran-
scendently glorious. The author was at Chefoo (China)
recuperating from sickness consequent on the strenu-
ous work of the medical missionary. He had agreed to
conduct a series of Bible addresses, and the subject
chosen was the coming of the Lord. For many years
he taught that Christ would return secretly to the air,
for His Church, that on earth the Great Tribulation
will follow the Rapture of the Church, that during the
Tribulation the Jews will be God's witnesses to the
world, and that several years after the secret coming
for the Church, our Lord, with His Church, will come
in manifested power and glory, to reign.

"Assured in his own mind that these were the
teachings of Scripture, he proceeded to prepare his
addresses by seeking for definite Bible declarations on
the subject. There was abundant and convincing proof
that Christ will come personally; but the Bible was

found to be silent regarding a secret coming, and silent as to any world missionary movement by the Jews until after Christ shall come in glory, and the veil of blindness be taken from Israel and the nations. Finally, to his consternation, he found there was no word about the Church being caught up before the Great Tribulation. Three texts upon which he had been relying to prove that the Church will not go through the Tribulation, showed on examination that they did not refer to the Tribulation.

"Feeling sick at heart at his inability to prove from the Bible what he believed to be the truth, he approached three senior missionaries, who like himself had taught these doctrines for about a quarter of a century (and who probably still teach them). He explained his difficulty and they kindly promised to help him. A few days later, each of the three regretfully admitted failure to find a single Scripture proof. In desperation he went to a resident missionary who was said to specialize in the study of prophecy. This friend said at once, 'There is no proof in the Bible of a secret coming, nor of the Church being taken away before the Great Tribulation, nor that the Church will escape the Great Tribulation'. This seemed confusing, but he promised to send a leaflet containing some of the thoughts of the late George Muller of Bristol. The leaflet arrived, but it made confusion worse confounded, for it said the Church must go through the Tribulation, since 2 Thessalonians 2 made it clear that Antichrist must be manifested before the coming of Christ, and our gathering together to Him in the air.

"During the following six months all the author's spare time was devoted to studying the Bible on this subject. During these months he relied as on a sheet anchor, upon the oft repeated saying, that because the Apostles and the early Church expected Christ would come in their day, therefore in our day we may expect Him to come at any moment. At length by diligently searching the Scriptures, with an earnest desire to learn what God had revealed, he found that his supposed sheet anchor was a chimera, and that the Apostles and the early Church did not expect Christ to come in their day, but contrariwise — Churches were warned that after the death of the Apostles Peter and Paul, they would pass through perilous times 'in the last days' of this age."

"Cling To My Bible"

Modern Church history acknowledges George Muller of Bristol as a very giant of godliness. This strong spiritual stalwart was a pronounced believer in Posttribulation-rapturism. It is recorded by Robert Cameron in his book, "Spiritual Truth About the Lord's Return": "When Mr. Muller was asked how it happened that he came to abandon the 'at any moment' expectation of the Lord's coming, and also the belief that the Church would escape the Great Tribulation he made a very prompt reply and said, 'My brother, I am a constant reader of my Bible and I soon found what I was taught to believe did not always agree with what my Bible said. I came to see that I must . . . cling to my Bible . . .'

"Never can I forget the wonderful Conference in the YMCA of Toronto, when over two hundred ministers sat on the platform every day while, in tenderness, he spoke of the unsearchable riches of Christ, and, in fiery indignation, of the evil of the present day, and also of the failure of the ministers to make known the coming of the Lord and their failure also to oppose the downgrade on which modern Christians had entered.

"He appealed to the ministers who had been preaching 'progress', and told them that just before us were horrible wars, famines, pestilences — the coming of the Antichrist, and the day of unequalled tribulation before the coming of our adorable Lord, Who alone could bring the day of peace. 'That', said he, 'is what you are coming to, and not the millennium of which you dream. Christ must come first to reward the saints and to crush His foes, but before He comes will occur the horrors of the Tribulation.' "

"Not Come Until the Apostasy"

Additional information concerning George Muller's Post-tribulation-rapture views is set forth in the statement: "Are we to expect our Lord's return at any moment, or that certain events must be fulfilled before He comes again". This was one of the nine questions answered by the late Mr. George Muller, at a public meeting held on Dec. 12, 1879, at Shaftesbury Hall, Toronto, Canada. His answer was: "I know that on this subject there is a great diversity of judgment, and I do not wish to force on other persons the light I have myself. The subject, however, is not new to me; for having been a careful, diligent student of the Bible for nearly fifty years, my mind has long been settled on this point, and I have not the shadow of a doubt about it. The Scriptures declare plainly that the Lord Jesus Christ will not come until the Apostasy shall have taken place, and the 'man of sin', the 'son of perdition' (or personal Antichrist) shall have been revealed as seen in 2 Thessalonians 2. Many other portions also of the Word of God distinctly teach that certain events are to be fulfilled before the return of our Lord Jesus Christ. This does not, however, alter the fact, that the coming of Christ, and not death, is the great hope of the church, and if in a right state of heart, we (as the Thessalonian believers did) shall 'serve the living and true God, and wait for His Son from heaven' ".

"Not One of Them"

Words from the pen of Robert Cameron are very appropriate: "If this novel view of Pre-tribulation rapture is anywhere taught in the Scripture, how did it escape the scrutiny of so many earnest students for eighteen centuries? The doctrine of the Lord's Return, and all kindred truths, occupied the attention of the Christian scholars very, very much during the first four centuries, but *not one of them* has betrayed any knowledge of the Church escaping the Tribulation. All of them, like Augustine, take the opposite view. See De Civitate Deo. Commenting on Daniel 7: 25 he says: 'He who reads this passage, even half-asleep, cannot fail to see that the Kingdom of Antichrist shall fiercely, though for a short time, assail the Church' ".

"Not From Holy Scripture"

A striking statement from the pen of S. P. Tregelles, who has been called "The greatest Biblical scholar of the nineteenth century in the British Empire" is here set forth for you to ponder: "I am not aware that there was any definite teaching that there would be a secret rapture of the Church at a secret coming until this was given forth as an utterance in Mr. Irving's Church from what was there received as being the voice of the Spirit. But whether anyone ever asserted such a thing or not, it was from that supposed revelation that the modern doctrine and the modern phraseology respecting it arose. *It came, not from Holy Scripture, but from that which falsely pretended to be the Spirit of God".*

CHAPTER NINE

"The Teaching Creates Problems"

During a recent extended Florida tour, two ministers, in different cities, said to me, using virtually the same words: "Mr. Scruby, could you enlighten me about the Rapture and the Tribulation? What does the Bible actually teach about the time of the Rapture? There are some passages that to me do not harmonize with the teaching I got at Bible school. The teaching of the Church's Rapture before the Tribulation creates problems that I cannot solve. What do you believe the Bible teaches?". These incidents have been multiplied many times across the nation through the years. It must be that the people are impressed by the omissions from my messages of the usual statements to the effect that "of course the Church will be raptured before the coming of Antichrist and the Tribulation".

No Scriptural Proof

Multitudes of such statements I have read; perhaps as many more I have heard. Never — *never, I say* — has anyone ever, in my reading, or hearing, ever attempted to follow such a statement with Scriptural proof. This must be significant. Is it that there is no proof? I believe so! Let me give you some actual sample statements, then you will see what I mean: "This spirit of antichrist is yet to culminate in a single personality whose identity will not be known by the Church, it having been raptured to heaven".

I have just concluded the reading of a book written by a friend on The Revelation. I give three statements made in the book. 1) "This generation which witnessed this ominous beginning of events leading to a supreme crisis, 'will not pass, till all these things be fulfilled'. But while the Church remains on earth up to the beginning of the Tribulation, it will not pass through it. Christ has promised that He will keep His Church from it, by coming to take it from the world." 2) "Finally it should be understood that when these events are being fulfilled the Church will have been raptured and will be with Christ in the heavens. No spiritual Christian will be left on earth to experience the awful persecutions and sufferings when Satan rules the world." 3) "This chapter constitutes a 'close-up' of the dominion of the beast and the false prophet of Revelation XIII. This cannot come while the Church is on earth."

Here are three positive, straight-forward assertions and not one of them is either preceded or followed by a single scratch of the pen to prove the contention. It is easy to understand why no Scripture proof is presented — simply because there is none! Again I say — assertion is not proof!

These quotations are typical. The bare statements are made and not one syllable of proof is offered. Readers of the assertions, including myself, are expected to accept them without question as being truth. To me assertion is not proof. I was born in London; my home is in Dayton; however, "I'm from Missouri". You have to "show me". Is that unreasonable? Well, that's the attitude the Bereans took.

"In the Clouds . . . In the Air"

Now let's make a simple, honest analysis of the first of these quotations. In the first place there is no statement in the Bible that the Church will be *"rap-*

tured to heaven". However, that the Church will be raptured at the second advent of Christ, is so stated by the Lord Himself. The teaching is included in the Olivetic discourse. The truth is vital. The language employed to explain it is lucid. Consider Christ's comments: "Immediately after the tribulation of those days . . . they shall see the Son of man coming in the clouds of heaven with power and great glory. . . . And He shall send His angels with a great sound of a trumpet, and they shall gather together His elect from the four winds, from one end of heaven to the other. . . . Then shall two be in the field; the one shall be taken, and the other left". Matthew 24: 31-40. Boldly Paul builds upon "the word of the Lord" as given by Christ in this sermon and He also contends that the Church "shall be caught up", or raptured. What he has to say about it is in 1 Thessalonians 4: 15-17. Will you read these words with me, just as they appear in the Bible? This, and nothing different, is what Paul says: "For this we say unto you by the word of the Lord [as spoken in the Olivetic sermon and recorded by Matthew], . . . For the Lord Himself shall descend from heaven . . . Then we which are alive and remain shall be caught up together with them *in the clouds,* to meet the Lord *in the air*: and so shall we ever be with the Lord". Since when did "to meet the Lord in *the air"* mean "raptured to heaven"? I ask this very sincerely, because, as a matter of simple logic, to me "meet the Lord *in the air"* does not mean *"raptured to heaven"*.

No Rapture In Revelation Four

Perhaps someone will say, "But what about John being caught up to heaven in Revelation 4: 1?". Yes, what about it? The Scofield Bible footnote says: "This call seems clearly to indicate the fulfilment of 1 Thessalonians 4:14-17".

Here, also is an example of exegesis I came across recently in a book on prophecy. The author declared: "The words, 'Come up hither', spoken by Jesus his Lord (Revelation 4:1) made him, who had been a partaker of Christ's sufferings become a partaker of His glory. Little intelligence is required to read the rapture of the saints in John's translation". Well, if "little intelligence is required to read the rapture of the saints in John's translation", then mine must be infinitesimal; indeed nil; as a matter of fact less than nothing — just a cipher with the rim rubbed out. I find it impossible, viewed in the light of Scripture and considered logic, to "read the rapture of the saints in John's translation".

There are some things decidedly wrong here. We are asked to "read in" something. That's the trouble with Pre-tribulation-rapture teaching — you have to "read in" too many things not actually there. This we should refuse to do. To do so may bring one dangerously near to being guilty of the evil against which we are warned in Revelation 22:18: "If any man shall *add unto these things,* God shall add unto Him the plagues that are written in this book".

Furthermore, the incident recorded in Revelation 4:1 is not the translation of John; and as a matter of fact has not the remotest relation to the Rapture. How many times must John be translated to heaven? Surely this cannot mean he was literally translated to heaven; for he states in the next verse: "Immediately I was in the *spirit*". If John's experience as recorded here is to be construed as a type of the Church's rapture, then John must be a type of the Church, and I am not aware this

is taught in the Scriptures. Also, the Rapture is not
to be a literal event because the apostle says: "I was
in the spirit" — that is only in spirit was he in heaven,
not actually, or in person. In a spiritual and not in a
literal sense, he was in heaven observing "things which
must be hereafter". If John's call to "come up hither"
typifies the Rapture of believers, then their rapture
will be only figurative, or spiritual, and not literal,
because John was not caught up to heaven actually,
but "in the spirit". Furthermore, the Church would
be raptured merely to be shown "things which must
be hereafter", for this is the specific reason why John
receives the call. I think it can be correctly said that
John in no sense here represents the Church, nor does
his visit to heaven "in the spirit" constitute "the rapture of the saints". If it does, then, a number of raptures are to be expected, because every similar circumstance in The Revelation must be regarded as typifying
a rapture. A number of such calls were issued to John
while he was receiving the Patmos vision. For instance,
we observe the same call coming to him in chapter six.
Taking it as we have the words in the Authorized
Version, then the call is issued four times. Each time
it is for a similar purpose as that stated in chapter four
— to behold, in vision, something about to occur. If
one call is to be understood to constitute a rapture of
the Church, then why not make all such calls represent a rapture of the Church? A very definite repetition of the scene in 4:1, 2 is shown in 17:1: "Come
hither; I will show unto thee . . .". Since we do not
have a weak cause to support, or a ridiculous fallacy
to sustain, I readily admit that in these subsequent
instances John is merely restating the situation that
appeared in chapter 1:10-12: "I was in the Spirit on
the Lord's day, and heard behind me a great voice, . . .

saying, . . . What thou seest write in a book". It is only that the circumstance was recurring.

Two Witnesses and the Rapture

Take a careful look at this. In Revelation 11 we find the amazing account of the two witnesses and their remarkable experiences during the Great Tribulation. "The beast . . . shall make war against them, and shall overcome them, and kill them. . . . And after three days and an half the spirit of life from God entered into them. . . . And they heard a great voice from heaven saying unto them, *Come up hither.* And they ascended up to heaven in a cloud: and their enemies beheld them". Now here is an occurrence that would more nearly typify the Rapture of the Church than the situation with John in 4: 1, 2. It certainly has more of the earmarks. I could more readily accept this as a type of the coming resurrection and rapture of the saints. To make it such — and there is much more reason for doing so than to make Revelation 4: 1 to represent the Church's rapture — would be to say that the Church will be in the Tribulation, will pass through it, and then be raptured. Observe that the two witnesses, having been persecuted by the Antichrist and then killed by him, are resurrected and called to "Come up hither" at the sounding of the seventh trumpet, which marks the end of the Tribulation. They participate therefore in the resurrection of the saints, described by John as "the first resurrection", Revelation 20: 5, 6, which resurrection of the bodies of believers is to take place "at the last trump". 1 Corinthians 15: 51, 52. Furthermore, their resurrection and rapture occur at the time of the coming of Christ to establish His kingdom (verse 15); and to reward His saints (verse 18). John states: "And the time of the dead [justified dead] that they should be judged, and that Thou shouldest give reward unto Thy servants the prophets, and to the saints, and them that fear Thy name, small and great". It was very clear to the Spirit-inspired apostle Paul that the "judgment of rewards" for saints will take place at the coming of Christ to set up His kingdom. Said he: "I charge thee therefore before God, and the Lord Jesus Christ, Who shall judge the quick [living] and the dead at His appearing [to establish] His kingdom". 2 Timothy 4:1. If this call to the two witnesses to "Come up hither" constitutes a type of the rapture, and very evidently it does, then it contradicts Pre-tribulation-rapturism.

The Church To See Antichrist

To continue the statement under consideration: it is observed the writer states — without offering any proof, because there is none — "this spirit of Antichrist is to culminate in a single personality whose identity will not be known by the Church, it having been raptured to heaven". This is stated in direct, and distressing contradiction of the one clear reference made by the apostle Paul concerning the relation of the Church to the coming Antichrist. Nothing could be set forth any more plainly than the facts as presented in 2 Thessalonians 2:1-3. It is one of the important prophetic passages to pour from the pen of the prince of preachers. We are to regard it as divinely inspired, therefore authentic and reliable.

Here, then, is exactly what is declared by God, and recorded by the apostle: "Now we beseech you, brethren, by the coming of our Lord Jesus Christ, and by our gathering together unto Him. That ye be not soon shaken in mind, or be troubled, neither by spirit, nor by word, nor by letter as from us, as that the day of

Christ is at hand. Let no man deceive you by any means: for that day shall not come, except there come a falling away first, and that man of sin be revealed, the son of perdition". In this prophetic utterance Paul tells of two personalities who are to come into the earth at the end of the age; and also speaks of two events that are to take place. 1) Christ is to come. It is stated in verse one: "The coming of our Lord Jesus Christ". 2) Antichrist will also be revealed. So we are assured in the words of verse three: "And that man of sin be revealed, the son of perdition". Two events are also scheduled to occur. 1) A falling away, or widespread apostasy is to develop as told in verse three: "Except there come a falling away first". 2) The second event spoken of in no uncertain terms is the rapture of the Church. This is very aptly stated as "our gathering together unto Him". Verse 1.

In a very clear statement, well understood by many to refer to the Lord's return and the Rapture, the writer pictures "our gathering together unto Him" by saying: "Then we which are alive and remain shall be caught up together in the clouds, to meet the Lord in the air". 1 Thessalonians 4: 17. This is "our gathering together unto Him" at "the coming of our Lord Jesus Christ". 2 Thessalonians 2: 1. This coming has already been vividly and dramatically described in the preceding chapter: "When the Lord Jesus shall be revealed from heaven with His mighty angels. . . . When He shall come to be glorified in His saints, and to be admired of all them that believe (because our testimony among you was believed) in that day". 2 Thessalonians 1: 7-10.

With such plain, God-inspired statements before us, what warrant has anyone for controverting them? and to assert that the "identity" of the Antichrist, the man of sin, "will not be known by the Church, it having been raptured to heaven". Here is precisely what the God-given word does say: "For that day [that is, the day of the coming of our Lord Jesus Christ, and our gathering together unto Him] shall not come, *except* there come a falling away first, and that man of sin be revealed, the son of perdition". How simple it all is when we take the words as given, and believe what they say — even if we don't like the conclusion offered. Here then is God's statement, clear and plain — the Rapture of the Church, at which time the believers will be gathered together unto Christ, shall not occur until after the great end-of-the-age apostasy has developed and produced the Antichrist, the man of sin. That the apostasy of the last days will produce the Antichrist is taught in this same passage, verse 10, "And with all deceivableness of unrighteousness in them that perish". The Antichrist will come in the midst of the great deceptions of the apostasy. If the false Christ is to be revealed before the revelation of Christ to Rapture His Church, then it most certainly is true that the Church *will* see, and know the Antichrist.

"The Abomination of Desolation"

Evidently Daniel by his reference to "the abomination that maketh desolate" has the Antichrist in mind. Our Lord in His Olivetic discourse spoke also of him to His disciples: "When ye therefore shall *see* the abomination of desolation, spoken of by Daniel the prophet, stand in the holy place". Daniel 12:11; Matthew 24:15. My principal reason, at the moment, for supposing that Jesus has Antichrist in mind when calling him the "abomination of desolation" is that Jesus informs us this person will stand "in the holy place".

Likewise, Paul informs us in 2 Thessalonians 2:4, that the Man of Sin "sitteth in the temple of God, showing himself that he is God". It is well understood by some that by his religious, social, political and economic abominations (deceptions) the Antichrist will bring spiritual desolation to the world. The point is, again, that Jesus reminds us that when events marking the last days of this age are taking place His followers would "see" the Antichrist; and to "see" him would be to identify him. Wouldn't you *rather* believe God than man? I would — and do.

Why the Warnings?

Another thing appears to me to be wrong with the teaching that the "identity [of the Antichrist] will not be known by the Church, it having been raptured to heaven". If this is true, why all the exhortations warning us to "watch", and "take heed", and to be on our guard against the deceptions and the delusions of the false Christ? Don't *you* too think all this is unnecessary and superfluous? it certainly is.

CHAPTER TEN

No Pre-tribulation-rapturism In Old Testament

To some who have been deceived by this false doctrine, it may seem strange, but actually there is no Pre-tribulation-rapture teaching in the Old Testament. I have made a prayerful and impartial study of the Old Testament Scriptures. They have been combed with a "fine tooth comb". Not one scratch of the pen has been found that could be construed as teaching, or even hinting at, a Rapture of the Church before the Tribulation. That the Tribulation is presented and pictured is certain. The return of the Lord is quite clearly spoken of. His return *with* His saints is as definitely and delightfully pictured. However, no Pre-tribulation-rapture is discovered anywhere in the Old Testament Scriptures.

Enoch and Prophets of Antiquity

Enoch impresses me as being a great saint. He stands in the Old Testament as a symbol of perfect sainthood. He represents perfect faith, trust, obedience, holiness and victory. He must also have been a great preacher. No man could be appointed and anointed of God and live as he lived without being a great preacher. After all, preaching is a matter of earnestness, not eloquence. It is a matter of sanctified conduct, not sentence construction. It is a matter of holy living, not homiletics. When God wanted to remind us of the great truth Enoch preached in his far-away day, He reached into the prophet's sermon barrel and brought out a sample sermon informing us "And Enoch also the seventh from

Adam, prophesied of these, saying, Behold, the Lord cometh with ten thousands of His saints". Jude 14. Here is a clear statement of the return of the Lord *with* His saints on the last day of the age when He appears in glory—nothing about His coming previously *for* them. It is to be noticed that "Enoch *also* prophesied". Well, if he *also* preached this, so did his contemporaries; as did those who went before, and those who came after him.

"All the Saints With Thee"

In the 14th chapter of his prophecy, Zechariah opens with the words: "Behold, the day of the Lord cometh". In very picturesque language he proceeds to describe it as "that day". It is evidently the last day of the age. "That day" as it ends, marks the consummation of an age and the commencement of a new dispensation. During "that day" a number of things transpire. Among them will be the coming of the Lord to earth in glory as promised. "And His feet shall stand in *that day* upon the mount of Olives. . . . And the Lord my God shall come and all the saints with thee." Zechariah 14: 4, 5. Nowhere in all the prophecy of Zechariah has anything been said about His having come previously to the air *for* the saints and remaining there, or returning to heaven for an extended stay that they might return later *with* Him. Why not? If true, should not something have been said about it somewhere? sometime? by someone?

God's People In The "Tribulation" But Not In The "Indignation"

In the most graphic terms the coming Great Tribulation of the end of this age is pictured in the Old Testament. Always, if the Church typified, is mentioned in reference to the time of trouble, it is shown to be in the midst of Tribulation conditions — and in some instances preserved therein by divine power. Never are they removed to escape trial or suffering until the end, or "Immediately after the tribulation", on the Day of the Lord. Removal by rapture is reserved for this specific day. Escape from the "indignation" of the "terrible" Day of the Lord is the heartening assurance given in Revelation 3:10. Fulfilment of this promise is not to be expected during the Tribulation proper.

Before we proceed further we might as well consider a passage recorded in Isaiah 26:20, 21. It may come to mind if readers are acquainted with the Pre-tribulation-rapture fallacy. "Well", says someone, "hasn't God promised that His people will escape tribulation? Isn't that what He is teaching here in the Old Testament? Yes, He has promised "escape", but not in the sense of being Raptured, or removed from the earth during the time of terrible tribulation. The words referred to read: "Come, My people, enter thou into thy chambers, and shut the doors behind thee: hide thyself as it were for a little moment, until the indignation be overpast. For behold, the Lord cometh out of His place to punish the inhabitants of the earth for their iniquity: the earth also shall disclose her blood, and shall no more cover her slain". This "little moment" is the Day of the Lord.

This is a God-given call. It shows the urgency of the situation and the seriousness of the "indignation" mentioned.

This may be intended to convey the thought that a refuge must be found by God's people during the fury of the "indignation" if they are to escape. It is evidently intended to convey the thought that a refuge will be provided for them during the fury of the indignation and the terrors of the Day of the Lord. It is just like our God to make such provision. There is still nothing to indicate that a Rapture of the saints to find sanctuary in heaven before the Tribulation has taken place. It is simply a command to "enter thou into thy chambers, and shut thy doors behind thee: *hide thyself as it were for a little moment*". This can be linked with the promise of our Lord in Revelation 3: 10: "Because thou hast kept the word of My patience, I also will keep thee from the hour of temptation, which shall come upon all the world, to try them that dwell upon the earth".

I am inclined to the opinion that the great, devastating, cataclysmic upheavals, featuring the destructive, apocalyptic forces so vividly described in Revelation 16: 17-21 will be held back until the "little moment" (short period) required at the age-end to work havoc on the earth. "And the seventh angel poured out his vial into the air; and there was a great voice out of the temple of heaven, . . . and there were thunders, and lightnings; and there was a great earthquake, . . . so mighty an earthquake. . . . And the great city was divided into three parts, and the cities of the nations fell: . . . And every island fled away, and the mountains were not found. And there fell upon man a great hail out of heaven, . . . And men blasphemed God because of the plague of the hail; for the plague thereof was exceeding great". It is to be noticed that these conditions exist only when the seventh vial is poured out, and the final seals are broken and the last of the trumpets are sounded. What John has written about these seems to point to the fact that the great, destructive fury will be confined to a "little moment" at the culmination of the Great Tribulation called the "Day of the Lord". Note what he writes in Revelation 6: 12-17: "And I beheld when he had opened the sixth seal, and, lo, there was a great earthquake; and the sun became black as sackcloth of hair, and the moon became as blood. And the stars of heaven fell unto the earth, even as a fig tree casteth her untimely figs, when she is shaken of a mighty wind. And the heaven departed as a scroll when it is rolled together; and every mountain and island were moved out of their places. And the kings of the earth, and the great men, and the rich men, and the chief captains, and the mighty men, and every bondman, and every free man, hid themselves in the dens and in the rocks of the mountains; and said to the mountains and rocks, Fall on us, and hide us from the face of Him that sitteth on the throne, and from the wrath of the Lamb: for the great day of His wrath is come; and who shall be able to stand?". Also read what John writes in Revelation 11: 13-19: "And the same hour was there a great earthquake, and the tenth part of the city fell, and in the earthquake were slain of men seven thousand: and the remnant were affrighted, and gave glory to the God of heaven. The second woe is past; and, behold, the third woe cometh quickly. And the seventh angel sounded; and there were great voices in heaven, saying, The kingdoms of this world are become the kingdoms of our Lord, and of His Christ; and He shall reign for ever and ever. And the four and twenty elders, which sat before God on their seats, fell upon their faces, and worshipped God, saying, We give Thee thanks, O Lord God Almighty, which art, and wast, and art to come; because Thou hast taken to Thee Thy great power, and hast reigned. And the nations were angry, and Thy wrath is come, and the time of the dead, that they should be judged, and that Thou shouldest give reward unto

Thy servants the prophets, and to the saints, and them that fear Thy name, small and great; and shouldest destroy them which destroy the earth. And the temple of God was opened in heaven, and there was seen in His temple the ark of His testament: and there were lightnings, and voices, and thunderings, and an earthquake, and great hail".

These passages indicate occurrences which obviously cover only a "little moment" or short time at the end of the Tribulation, known as the "Day of the Lord". To assure survival during the apparent widespread destruction of that time it will be necessary to be removed from the midst of it, hence the command, "hide thyself as it were for a little moment", and the promise, "I also will keep thee from the hour of temptation".

When Jesus spoke of the Great Tribulation, He told of its certainty, saying: "For then shall be great tribulation". Matthew 24: 21. He also indicated its brevity, declaring: "And except those days should be shortened . . . for the elect's sake those days shall be shortened". Matthew 24: 22. I think it is clear that Jesus did not mean that the divinely pre-determined duration of the Tribulation will be altered and curtailed, but only that, in His wisdom and mercy, God decided in advance that the period should be very brief. When telling of the Great Tribulation, Christ emphasized the dreadful character of it. He made direful predictions about the Tribulation, showing that it will be featured by distressing conditions and dreadful consternation. Jesus said: "And great earthquakes shall be in divers places, and famines, and pestilences; and fearful sights and great signs shall be from heaven. . . . And there shall be signs in the sun, and in the moon, and in the stars; and upon the earth distress of nations, with perplexity; the sea and the waves roaring; men's hearts failing them for fear, and for looking after those things which are coming on the earth; for the powers of heaven shall be shaken". Luke 21: 11, 25, 26. Literally translated, these words reveal that the character of the Tribulation will be such that nations will be dismayed and men will swoon with fear, and foreboding, and panic, and dread, because of what threatens the universe. And well they might, because Jesus said: "For then shall be great tribulation, such as was not from the beginning of the world to this time, no, nor ever shall be. And except those days should be shortened, there should no flesh be saved". Matthew 24: 21, 22. The point to be noticed here is the significant fact, that this dread-filled period will be climaxed by globe-rocking, universe-changing cataclysmic conditions. Jesus said: *Immediately after the tribulation of those days* shall the sun be darkened, and the moon shall not give her light, and the stars shall fall from heaven, and the powers of the heavens shall be shaken". The only future advent of Christ predicted in the Scriptures is scheduled to occur at this point, for, "Immediately after the tribulation [when these dreadful and devastating events are taking place] . . . then shall appear the sign of the Son of man . . . and they shall see the Son of man coming . . . and . . . shall gather together His elect". Matthew 24: 29-31. They are the "elect" of the Son, for Christ specified "His" elect.

The "Day Of The Lord" And The "Indignation"

The Great Tribulation will end with the Day of the Lord. In other words, the Day of the Lord is not to be regarded as synonymous with the Great Tribulation. It is only the climax thereof. It seems clear from the Scriptures that it covers only one day — the final day of the age. On this day "the Lord will take vengeance

enemies. . . . The Lord hath His way in the whirlwind
and the storm, and the clouds are the dust of His feet.
. . . The mountains quake at Him, and the hills melt,
and the earth is burned at His presence, yea, the world,
and all that dwell therein. Who can stand before His
INDIGNATION? and who can abide the fierceness of
His anger? His fury is poured out like fire, and the
rocks are thrown down by Him. . . . He will make an
utter end of the place thereof". Nahum 1:2-8. This is
a sample of the terrible threats uttered by the Lord
against the wicked to be carried out on the Day of
the Lord. This passage tells of the poured-out fury of
the Lord in the Day of His "indignation". No wonder
He inquires, regarding the terrible visitation of the
Day of the Lord: "Who can stand before His indignation? and who can abide the fierceness of His anger?".
The answer is found in the words of Christ's promise
in Revelation 3:10: "Because thou hast kept the word
of My patience, I also will keep thee from the hour of
temptation, which shall come upon all the world, to try
them that dwell upon the earth". Those who have
patiently kept His word, will be rewarded by being
kept from the dreadful day when He takes vengeance
upon the wicked in His indignation. They will be kept
from these swift and overwhelming judgments of the
Day of the Lord, by being "caught up . . . in the clouds,
to meet the Lord in the air".

The Day of the Lord is spoken of many times in the
Scriptures. Joel speaks of the Day of the Lord in
chapter two, verse one, of his prophecy, and then proceeds to give a very vivid description of events that
occur on the final day of this age, including the Battle
of Armageddon. He is careful to stress the point in
verse two that it is "a day" — one day.

Zechariah also, in chapter fourteen, verse one, mentions the Day of the Lord. He also goes on to describe in graphic words, events that transpire on the last day of this age, and lists, too, the Battle of Armageddon. He emphasizes the fact that it is "one day". Many other such references could be given. Various translators have supported the clear meaning relative to the duration of the Day of the Lord. Rotherham renders it thus: "It shall be one day by itself"; Leeser, the Jewish scholar, says: "It shall be one particular day".

"Alas for the day! for the *Day of the Lord* is at hand, and as a destruction from the Almighty shall it come. . . . For the *Day of the Lord* is great and very terrible; and who can abide it?" Joel 1:15; 2:11. Mind you, these Scriptures do not describe the Great Tribulation, but its closing day, the *Day of the Lord*. It is to be noticed that corresponding descriptions of this day are contained in both the Old and the New Testaments. The Old Testament account runs thus: "And I will show wonders in the heavens and in the earth, blood, and fire, and pillars of smoke. The sun shall be turned into darkness, and the moon into blood, before the great and the terrible *Day of the Lord come*". Joel 2:30, 31. Similar dramatic descriptions of the Day of the Lord are given in such passages as Isaiah 2:12-21; 13: 1-10; 34:1-8; Zephaniah 1:14-18; Haggai 2:6-23. Christ's own account, from the Olivetic discourse, parallels this: "*Immediately after the tribulation of those days* [*on the Day of the Lord*] shall the sun be darkened, and the moon shall not give her light, and the stars shall fall from heaven, and the powers of the heavens shall be shaken". Matthew 24:29. The Revelation record runs true to form: "And the seventh angel poured out his vial into the air, and there came a great voice out of the temple of heaven, from the throne, saying, *It is*

done. And there were voices, and thunders, and lightnings; and there was a great earthquake, such as was
not since men were upon the earth, so mighty an earthquake, and so great". Revelation 16:17, 18.

The Day of the Lord will be a day of conjunction.
It will be a day of transition. Coming "Immediately
after the tribulation" it will actually end the age and
will join it onto the next age. It will mark the transition from the grace age to the kingdom age. The Rapture of the Church is scheduled to occur on that day —
the Day of the Lord. On that fateful day, judging from
all the Scriptures describing it, the pent-up fury of the
long-suffering and outraged Almighty will surge up in
a great sweep of judgment wrath against the wicked.
Few of the wicked shall "escape". All the physical
universe will be caught in this convulsive, cataclysmic,
climactic judgment blow. "Behold, the Lord maketh
the earth empty, and maketh it waste, and turneth it
upside down, and scattereth abroad the inhabitants
thereof. . . . The land shall be utterly emptied, and
utterly spoiled. . . . Therefore hath the curse devoured
the earth, and they that dwell therein are desolate;
therefore the inhabitants of the earth are burned and
few men left." Isaiah 24:1-6. In one "hour" of that day
of frightful devastation the blow will fall; "and few
men [will be] left". That "hour" will witness the fulfilment of the glorious promise of Revelation 3:10. The
gracious provision made for God's people will be realized in their r e m o v a l from the earth to "escape"
the Day of the Lord judgments by rapture. For has
He not promised: "Because thou hast kept the word
of My patience, I also will keep thee from *the hour*
of temptation, which shall come upon all the world to
try them that dwell upon the earth"? When is this to
take place? "Immediately *after* the tribulation" and

"*before* the great and terrible Day of the Lord come".
Matthew 24: 29;　Joel 2: 31.

This claim is supported by all the types in the Old
Testament that have any relation to the Great Tribulation and the Day of the Lord. There are two series
of types that fall into these categories. The Tribulation
types present aspects that correspond to the New Testament teaching concerning it. Typical Antichrists are
seen. Persecution is pictured, etc. In every instance,
such as the Hebrew children in the fiery furnace; Israel
in Egypt; Elijah in Jezreel, the Church is represented
as "escaping" by survival in the midst of the Tribulation conditions. In such conditions the Church "endures
unto the end".

A second series may be classified as Day of the Lord
types. No persons standing for the Antichrist appears
in these types. There is no reference to persecution.
The general outline shows evil conditions. The Church,
typified by one, or more persons, is in the midst of these
conditions. In each case this extended period of great
wickedness ends with a swift, retributive, devastating
judgment-blow that works great havoc upon the physical world and suffering and death upon the world
dwellers; but, and this is the important thing to note,
the righteous are always removed on the day, indeed
in the very "hour", the judgment-blow descends. There
is no variation from the principle established in all
these Day of the Lord types. Jesus brought out this
truth in His teaching concerning Lot and the destruction of the cities of the plain by fire; also in the story
of Noah and the destruction of the world by flood. Always, without exception the principle shown is *preservation* in the trials of days of Tribulation, and *removal*
from the judgments of the Day of the Lord.

"The Same Day Lot Went Out Of Sodom"

Consider the case of Lot first. "Likewise also as it was in the days of Lot; they did eat, they drank, they bought, they sold, they planted, they builded; *but the same day Lot went out of Sodom it rained fire and brimstone from heaven and destroyed them all.*" Luke 17: 28, 29. The city of Sodom was doomed. Judgment was pronounced. "For we will desert this place. . . . Then the Lord rained upon Sodom and Gomorrah brimstone and fire. . . . And He overthrew those cities and all the plains and all the inhabitants of the cities, and that which grew upon the ground." Genesis 19: 13, 24, 25. Righteous Lot and his family lived in Sodom. It was God's desire for them to escape the judgment fire and great destruction. The urgent message came from the Lord: "ESCAPE for thy life; . . . ESCAPE *to the mountains,* lest thou be consumed". Genesis 19: 17. Even a casual glance at this narrative will show that Lot did ESCAPE. He ESCAPED by removal. He was mercifully, and miraculously, and literally delivered "out of the midst of the overthrow". Genesis 19: 29. Judgment fire and brimstone fell in widespread destruction upon all the cities of the plain. Visitation of divine judgment-wrath was felt upon the wicked. *"The same day Lot went out of Sodom* it rained fire and brimstone from heaven and destroyed them all." He ESCAPED by being "caught up" "to the mountain". Truly we see the promise fulfilled: "I also will keep thee from the hour of temptation [trial]". The type is perfect. The interpretation is easy. The implication is clear and conclusive. Post-tribulation-rapture is its teaching.

"The Day That Noah Entered . . . The Flood Came"

The removal-promise for the Day of the Lord is adequately demonstrated in all Old Testament types. Noah and his family are representative of the saved family of God—"the household of faith". The devastation by the flood clearly speaks of the judgment time of "the *hour* of temptation [testing], which shall come upon all the world". Revelation 3:10. The ark is known to be a very apt type of Christ the Saviour. He is our refuge.

Some facts in the story of the great deluge stand out in bold relief. Noah had been aware for a long time of the impending judgment-disaster. The hour of deluge-doom approached. Before the hour of doom struck God notified Noah of it seven days in advance. God prepared the patriarch by saying: *"For yet seven days, . . .* And every living substance that I have made will I destroy from off the face of the earth". The command to build the ark and instructions for preparing it had been previously given. Its construction was completed. The judgment-day loomed. As it approached, to make sure that there would be ample time to load the ark with its cargo of creatures and supplies for them, God set the seven-days' deadline for the deluge. The task of loading the boat would be tremendous. Anyone who has seen animals loaded on ships will readily realize the magnitude of this undertaking. A prolonged stay in the ark by such a company of humans and animals would require a large supply of provisions. This great undertaking of loading the animals and stowing these supplies occupied the time of Noah and the seven other members of his family for the whole of the seven days. There could be no lost moments. The years of my boyhood were spent, among other things, watching the loading and unloading of ships. I know that even with modern mechanical equipment, and trained and efficient stevedores such a task as Noah faced would be a big one, but it was even more arduous because he had only man-power, and a very limited amount too, to depend upon for the work. Let's read of what constituted the cargo of the ark: "And thou shalt come into the ark, thou, and thy sons, and thy wife, and thy sons' wives with thee. And of every living thing of all flesh, two of every sort shalt thou bring into the ark, ... of fowls after their kind, of every creeping thing of the earth after his kind, two of every sort shall come unto thee, ... And take thou unto thee of all food that is eaten, and thou shalt gather it to thee; and it shall be for food for thee, and for them. Thus did Noah; according to all that God commanded him, so did he". Genesis 6:18-22. What busy days those must have been for all of Noah's family; for it was not until the seven-day period commenced that the command came from the Lord to load the animals and provisions into the ark. Every waking hour must have been occupied with the multiplicity of chores. Hustle was the order of each and every day. "And it came to pass *after seven days,* that the waters of the flood were upon the earth. ... *In the selfsame day entered Noah,* ... the sons of Noah, and Noah's wife, and the three wives of his sons with them, into the ark; ... And the waters increased, and bare up the ark, *and it was lift up above the earth"*. Genesis 7:10-17. Noah and his family found it necessary to make a very hasty entry into the ark because of the sudden surge of the waters. Days of feverish activity were ended. With their task completed they dare not linger but were apparently forced to rush breathless "into the ark, *because of the waters of the flood"*. That they were compelled to hurry ahead of the threatening waters and thus escape into the ship at the last moment is suggested by various renderings of Genesis 7:7. Rotherham claims: "So Noah entered, and his sons and his wife and his sons' wives with him into the ark — *from before the waters of the flood"*. Moffat states: *"At the end of the seven days* the waters of the deluge covered the earth; and Noah went into the barge along with his sons and wife and his sons' wives, *driven by the waters of the deluge"*.

When were the sluice-gates of heaven opened, and the fountains of the deep broken up bringing the great earth-covering, destructive, death-dealing deluge? *"After [the] seven days."* Verses 4, 10. At what time did Noah and his family, by entering the ark, seek and find deliverance from the disaster that followed? *"In the selfsame day."* Verse 13. *At the end of the seven day period, not at the beginning.* What happened to the ark and its occupants during this day of destruction? "The waters increased, and bare up the ark, *and it was lifted up above the earth."* Verse 17. Was the ark, which typified Christ: and Noah's family, who are a type of the Christians, the family of God "in Christ", raptured to heaven? No, they were "lifted up above the earth", and so away from the destruction and death. They "escaped the [spiritual] corruption that is [was] in the world" during the antediluvian period, and were preserved physically during the flood, by being "kept by the power of God through faith". 2 Peter 1:4; 1 Peter 1:5. This will be repeated in the experience of saints during the Great Tribulation when there will be a repetition of the "days of Noah". They were permitted to "escape" the fearful and fateful forces of the flood as it broke in its judgment fury upon the wicked world, by being "lifted up above the earth" "after [the] seven days". Thus, a later promise, made to "Day of the Lord" saints, was realized by "Days of Noah" believers. God has promised: "I also will keep thee from the hour of temptation [trial], which shall come upon all them that dwell upon the earth". Revelation 3:10.

Noah and his family, in the ark, were "lifted up above the earth" "after [the] seven days". Saints who are of the "household of faith" in Christ, the ark of salvation, "shall be caught up . . . to meet the Lord in the air", "Immediately after the tribulation" on the "Day of the Lord". Genesis 7: 4-17; Matthew 24: 29-31; 1 Thessalonians 4: 16, 17; 5: 2. How could the facts be clearer? They should drive us from the fallacy of Pre-tribulation-rapturism. We are to be "kept", not by being taken "out of the world" during the Great Tribulation and the reign of the Antichrist; Jesus desires that God do something more remarkable, and certainly more miraculous. He wants that we should be "kept" in the midst of the evil. This appeals to the heroic and chivalrous in one. Pre - tribulation - rapturism is too soft and flabby for men of God who are exhorted: "Thou therefore *endure hardness* as a good soldier of Jesus Christ". 2 Timothy 2: 3. It is too anemic. It is a body with the blood drained out. It leaves little, or no strength to "Fight the good fight of faith", and to "lay hold on eternal life". 1 Timothy 6: 12.

"He That Shall Endure Unto the End"

Noah's faith fortified him, and carried him through the seven days. Diligently he worked until the flood came. *He endured to the end.* A coming time of "sorrows" is pictured by Christ as He mounts His Olivetic pulpit. Tribulation conditions are graphically portrayed. End-of-the-age conditions are faithfully described. The tremendously significant and heartening promise is added: *"But he that shall endure unto the end, the same shall be saved".* Matthew 24: 13. The "end" referred to here is the same "end" mentioned in the succeeding verse, "And then shall the end come". *It is the full end of the age.* "Then shall be great tribu-

lation" including war, pestilence, famine, earthquakes,
persecution, hatred, and other evils and satanic forces
that bring widespread suffering and death. *"He that
shall endure unto the end* [*of the age — including the
period of the Great Tribulation —*] *the same shall
be saved"* from physical death. "THEN [*at the end
of the Tribulation*] *we which are alive and remain
shall be caught up . . . to meet the Lord in the air."*
The story of Noah and his family, with nothing deleted
or added, is a perfect type, teaching "escape" by Rapture at the end of the Tribulation, on the Day of the
Lord.

"When I Smite the Land of Egypt"

Now I ask you to consider an Old Testament narrative which is a combination Tribulation and Day of
the Lord type. Types are not given to teach truth, but
they are certainly given to support, and perhaps to
clarify doctrine. Israel is a type. Because a thing cannot be a type of itself, she could not be a type of herself,
just as, for instance, Christ could not be a type of Himself. National Israel is a type of spiritual Israel, the
Church. Israel was temporarily in the land of Egypt
which is a type of the unspiritual, hostile world. The
Church finds itself "in the world" although "not of the
world". The world is unspiritual and hostile. Israel
was held in bondage and was severely treated because a powerful king feared their power and opposed
them: "Therefore they did set over them taskmasters
to afflict them with their burdens. . . . And they made
their lives bitter with hard bondage, . . . wherein they
made them serve". Exodus 1: 11, 14. At the end of this
age will come an all-powerful, Satan-inspired, devil-
empowered ruler, known as Antichrist. He will attempt
to exercise absolute control over all thrones and gov-

ernments and all the people of that time. The people
of Israel honored God above Pharaoh and so were
brutally mistreated. Many of God's people will decline
to worship and obey the Antichrist and so will be
greatly tried during a period known as the Great Tribulation.

However, the story of Israel in Egypt ends right.
God sent upon the land a series of ten judgment
plagues that caused widespread death and unprecedented suffering to the Egyptians. In the providence
of God none of the plagues affected the Israelites.
Though in the midst of them, they were nevertheless
protected from their deadly effects. Then one day the
army of the Egyptian king was utterly destroyed so
there "remained not so much as one of them". Exodus
14:28. *That very day when the great and evil ruler
and his army was utterly destroyed, all the children
of Israel were delivered* — "Then the Lord saved Israel
that day out of the hands of the Egyptians". Exodus
14:30. It was a case of redemption from sin by the
blood and deliverance from tribulation by the "arm
of the Lord", the miraculous "power of His might".
"For I will pass through the land of Egypt this night,
and will smite the firstborn in the land of Egypt, both
man and beast; and against all the gods of Egypt I
will execute judgment; I am the Lord. . . . *And the
plague shall not be upon you to destroy you, when I
smite the land of Egypt.*" Exodus 12:12, 13.

Keep in mind the Israelites were in the land and
were not removed from it, until the end of the period
of wrath and judgment. The Church will be in the
world to pass through the Great Tribulation. To any
mind not blinded by prejudice, or seared by unbelief,
brought on by a deadly fallacy, the application should
be clear. Throughout the entire period of bondage,

including the time of tribulation and plagues, the Israelites were in the land of Egypt. *They endured unto the end.* They were not removed at any period prior to the full end of the judgment time. The very same day — indeed the same "hour" (Rev. 3:10) the tyrannical king, and his evil army were destroyed — that's when the people of God gained deliverance. This all came about through the blood of sacrifice and the power of God. If language in Scripture has a specific meaning, then it is clear that *the Church will pass through the entire period of Tribulation, and will be Raptured at the very end.* When the wicked and false Christ, with his devil-driven army are destroyed, then deliverance will come to the Church.

"I, Even I Only, Am Left"

God always matches desperate conditions with dedicated Christians. Whenever conditions are unusually bad God raises up good men, saves them by His grace, fills them with the Holy Spirit and clothes them with the Spirit's power, then thrusts them into the midst of these evil conditions and enables them to live strong, radiant, victorious lives, and so proves it is possible for anyone, anywhere, anytime to be a genuine Christian. This is the meaning we gather from the story of Elijah the prophet of God. He lived at a time when a wicked, despotic king was upon the throne. Ahab opposed God. He r e q u i r e d all to worship Baal. Many refused. Among them was Elijah. He felt it necessary to flee from the wrath of the outraged ruler. It was proper that he should. Matt. 10:23; 4:12; 12:15. He sought refuge in obscurity. God visited him because he became depressed in his predicament and was overwhelmed by a feeling of utter loneliness. The evil king had his fingers at the throat of everything sacred.

Every holy thing was being throttled. Wickedness had come to flood-tide. Iniquity abounded. Altars of God were being demolished. People of God were being persecuted. Men of God were being martyred. Elijah considered himself to be a lone survivor. From his discouraged heart poured the bitter lamentation: "I, even I only, am left; and they seek my life to take it away". 1 Kings 19:10.

God informed him there was a large and noble army of seven thousand compatriots who had not obeyed the king's decree. At a time when food was difficult to procure by those who held out against the decree from the throne, God fed Elijah miraculously. By divine intervention, and miraculous provision, the man of God was able "to endure unto the end" *and then "went up by a whirlwind into heaven".* Perhaps the seven thousand were also fed miraculously and were preserved by divine power. It may be assumed that the experience of one was the experience of all.

Boycott and the Mark of the Beast

"As it was . . . so shall it be." The Antichrist, a "king of fierce countenance", will occupy the throne of world power for a brief period at the end of this age. He will exercise monopolistic control over thrones and governments and all organizations, religious and secular. He will institute a universal system of boycott. Everyone will be forbidden to "buy or sell" without his consent. To secure this, it will be necessary to acknowledge and worship him, and to unite with his organization, and receive the mark, or emblem, which will be the insignia of membership.

It is obvious that the story of Elijah is a type. Elijah and the seven thousand in that far-away day were not taken out of the world. They were there on earth to face the wicked king, and were subject to his evil decrees. In the Great Tribulation, when the coming Man of Sin holds evil dominion over the earth, the Church will be present to face him. Christians will be affected by his reign of terror and will be subject to his edicts. Just as Elijah and the host of faithful souls survived that time of Great Tribulation, and thus *endured unto the end,* so are many destined to do under the reign of Antichrist. In the 13th and 14th chapters of The Revelation, John tells of the Great Tribulation; the activities of the Antichrist; the coming of the mark of the beast, and its direful consequences, then significantly adds — by divine direction, mind you: "Here is the patience of the saints; here are they that keep the commandments of God, and the faith of Jesus". Revelation 14: 12. The word patience is the same as the word endurance. Actually, John is saying: "When the Antichrist comes, and the mark of the beast is being imprinted upon people, that's when the saints will need endurance. They will need endurance to do two things. First, to obey God rather than Antichrist. Second, to keep faith with Jesus.

There follows a special message from our Lord to His Church for Tribulation times. This is not primarily a funeral text, it is a promise telling the blessedness of even martyrdom *during the Great Tribulation.* "And I heard a voice from heaven saying unto me, Write, Blessed are the dead which *die in the Lord from henceforth:* yea, saith the Spirit that they may rest from their labours and their works do follow them." Especially blessed are they who die, rather than yield to the soul-damning decrees of the Antichrist. The word *henceforth* is the pivotal word. "Henceforth" — after the mark of the beast begins.

"A Thousand Shall Fall At Thy Side"

I have pondered the words of Psalm 91. It would not violate the Scripture itself, neither would it be necessary to resort to fanciful and forced interpretation, to say that the Psalm seems to give a preview of the "fearful sights and great signs" that shall prevail on the earth during the Great Tribulation. It includes the promise of divine protection in the midst of frightful plagues and fearful powers. Many of the Godless will be stricken. Evil men shall be destroyed. To His people God affirms: "A thousand shall fall at thy side, and ten thousand at thy right hand; but it shall not come nigh thee. Only with thine eyes shalt thou behold and see the reward of the wicked". Extended comment is unnecessary. It only needs to be said that if the wicked *"shall fall at thy side, and . . . at thy right hand;"* and if "with thine eyes shalt thou behold and see the reward of the wicked" then — all of the Pre-tribulation - rapture theories notwithstanding — the righteous must be present in the midst of the Tribulation conditions. However, in this case, they are miraculously preserved — and for a good reason, for the psalmist adds: "Because thou hast made the Lord, which is my refuge, even the most High, thy habitation; there shall no evil befall thee, neither shall any plague come nigh thy dwelling". They *do* have their "dwelling" in the Tribulation. They *are* "delivered" because they "dwell in the secret place of the most High" and "abide under the shadow of the Almighty". "The Lord" is their "refuge" and their "fortress" while they are on the earth. There is no Rapture promised in order to escape Tribulation. They "escape" by being "kept" in their "refuge". It is interesting and significant that the United States government in literature giving instructions as to what to do in the event of an atomic attack, urges this one, all important rule, "Get Shielded". In other words, find a refuge.

The Psalm gives not only a probable preview of the Tribulation, and the protection afforded the righteous so they are preserved in the troublous times, but sets forth a never-failing principle of the spiritual realm. *God grants protection and promises preservation in the midst of trial, and that on the basis of His grace and mercy, and we are living in Him Who is "The secret place" and the "ark" of salvation.* This principle is amply vouched for by Paul in 1 Corinthians 10:13: "There hath no temptation [trial] taken [overtaken] you but such as is common to man: but God is faithful, Who will not suffer you to be tempted [tested] above that ye are able; but will with the temptation also make a way to escape, *that ye may be able to bear it*". "*Escape*" by survival; not "*escape*" by removal before the Tribulation — that is the prevailing principle in Scripture.

Beloved reader, search where you will, but nowhere, will you find any statement in the Old Testament Scriptures that even remotely hints at a Pre-tribulation-rapture. It has to be "read in" Scripture, and both text and type, must be woefully and wilfully "wrested", misinterpreted and misapplied. If there is to be a Rapture before the Tribulation, I think as a matter of fairness to us, it should at least be hinted at in the Old Testament somewhere; in someway.

CHAPTER ELEVEN
Rapture and Revelation

Jesus proclaimed the fact of His second coming. He preached of it while on earth. He would "come again", He said. When, however, did He ever say He would come "*for*" His saints, and then later "*with*" His saints? The answer is—nowhere! This is a man-made expression to support a purely fictional fallacy. The dividing of the *second* coming into *three, or more* comings is advocated on hypothetical grounds. Its advocates are among those who cherish a religion of sentiment. Much of the mystery that surrounds the story of "the missing Christians" is unscriptural imagery. It makes fancy preaching, but it ignores evident facts.

In 1916 an acquaintance published a book on The Revelation. I have just re-read it. On page 113 I find the statement: "If Jesus should come for His Church today — and there is no unfulfilled scripture between us and that event but God's longsuffering mercy". This dear man some time later went to glory. I have often wondered what he would say now if he should be aware of all that has taken place since 1916. At least he would see the absurdity of his statement.

In 1918 I heard a very dear friend, while preaching parrot-like on the second coming of Christ, make this same statement. He still lives, and because his dogmatic declaration proved to be as untrue as absurd, he has abandoned the dispensational view of Scripture. He had heard a number of able preachers tell of how Jesus would come "*for*" His saints, then later come "*with*" His saints. Gullibility seems to stultify intellect-

uality. My friend did not analyze this "sweet morsel"
of present-day prophetic preaching. Had he done so,
and then tested it by the teachings of God's Word, he
would have learned that it is a mere sophistry. It is
not Scriptural. It is unscriptural and antiscriptural.
It no doubt appealed to him as being profound — so,
like many others, he expounded it. Said he, one day
in my hearing: "The second coming will be, as it were,
in two sections. Christ will come *for* His saints and
then *with* His saints". He then attempted to illustrate
the alleged two-fold coming of Christ by saying: "I
recently rode on a train that ran in two sections". So
what? I have ridden on trains — especially during the
war days — that ran in as many as three or four sections. But there will not be three or four "comings"
of Christ. Each train, despite all we may make out of
it, is a separate and different train and each carries a
different company.

If the second coming is to be two events, then certainly Jesus should have said as much. He should at
least have said *something* that could be so construed.
Did He? Evidently not! Just what did He say? Nothing that could mean that He would come in secret
to Rapture His saints, and then be revealed openly
with them at some subsequent time. This He *never*
taught. Consult the four gospels. Compare the many
conclusive, clear statements the Lord made, with the
few hazy passages some have seized upon as teaching
the two-fold coming.

Shall we take Christ's first statement as recorded in
Matthew's Gospel? "The Son of man shall come in the
glory of His Father with His angels; and then shall He
reward every man according to His works". Matthew
16:27. No secret coming or secret rapture there. Put
by the side of that His assertion: "And then shall they

see the Son of Man coming in a cloud *with power and great glory*". Luke 21:27. Nor is there any secret coming and secret rapture in these words! Now add this declaration: "Wherefore if they say unto you, Behold, He is in the desert; go not forth: behold, He is in the secret chambers; believe it not. *For as the lightning cometh* out of the East and shineth even unto the West; so shall also the coming of the Son of man be". Now, how can one see a secret coming and rapture in these statements of the Saviour?

"Then Shall"

These passages are thoroughly representative. There is no contrary passage from the lips of the Master. Without attempting any fancy interpretation; without "reading in" anything; without attempting to force Scriptures to fit a false theory; without putting the Jew where the Church quite evidently belongs; refraining from grasshopper exegesis; avoiding the practice of jumping from passage to passage — in short let us be content to take the words of our Lord as they are recorded by Matthew, taken from His Olivetic discourse. Now here is what we learn from Jesus Himself about the matter of His coming in relation to the Great Tribulation as told in chapters twenty-four and twenty-five of Matthew's Gospel:

Verse 9. "*THEN SHALL* they deliver you up to be afflicted, and shall kill you; and ye shall be hated of all nations for My name's sake.

10. And *THEN SHALL* many be offended, and shall betray one another, and shall hate one another.

11. And many false prophets SHALL rise, and SHALL deceive many.

12. And because iniquity SHALL abound, the love of many SHALL wax cold.

13. But he that SHALL endure unto the end, the same SHALL be saved.

14. And this gospel of the kingdom SHALL be preached in all the world for a witness unto all nations; and *THEN SHALL* the end come.

21. For *THEN SHALL* be great tribulation, such as was not since the beginning of the world, to this time, no, nor ever shall be.

22. And except those days should be shortened, there should no flesh be saved; but for the elect's sake those days SHALL be shortened.

27. For as the lightning cometh out of the east and shineth even unto the west; so SHALL also the coming of the Son of Man be.

29. IMMEDIATELY AFTER THE TRIBULATION OF THOSE DAYS SHALL the sun be darkened, and the moon shall not give her light, and the stars SHALL fall from heaven, and the powers of the heavens SHALL be shaken;

30. AND THEN SHALL APPEAR THE SIGN OF THE SON OF MAN in heaven; and THEN SHALL all the tribes of the earth mourn, and THEY SHALL SEE THE SON OF MAN COMING IN THE CLOUDS OF HEAVEN WITH POWER AND GREAT GLORY.

31. And He SHALL send His angels with a great sound of a trumpet, and they SHALL gather together His elect from the four winds [i.e., from "the air"], from one end of heaven to the other.

40. THEN SHALL TWO BE IN THE FIELD; THE ONE SHALL BE TAKEN, AND THE OTHER LEFT.

41. Two women SHALL be grinding at the mill; the one SHALL be taken, and the other left.

42. Watch therefore; for ye know not what hour your Lord doth come.

25:1. THEN SHALL the kingdom of heaven be likened unto ten virgins which took their lamps, and went forth to meet the bridegroom.

31. When the Son of man SHALL COME IN HIS GLORY, and all the holy angels with Him, THEN SHALL HE SIT UPON THE THRONE OF HIS GLORY.

34. THEN SHALL the king say unto them on His right hand, Come, ye blessed of My Father, inherit the kingdom prepared for you from the foundation of the world.

37. THEN SHALL the righteous answer Him saying, Lord, when saw we Thee an hungred, and fed Thee? or thirsty, and gave Thee drink?

41. THEN SHALL He say unto them on the left hand, Depart from Me, Ye cursed, into everlasting fire, prepared for the devil and his angels:

44. THEN SHALL they answer Him, saying, Lord, when saw we Thee an hungred, or athirst, or a stranger, or naked, or sick, or in prison, and did not minister unto Thee?

45. THEN SHALL He answer them, saying, Verily I say unto you, Inasmuch as ye did it not to one of the least of these, ye did it not to Me.

I have quoted at length for the sake of clarity and emphasis. These words are from the Olivetic sermon preached by Jesus. It will be noted that "THEN SHALL" is used fourteen times. These are the words of continuity. They show various events in sequence. The facts are quite clearly stated. These events occur in connection with the Great Tribulation — and "IMMEDIATELY AFTER THE TRIBULATION . . . SHALL APPEAR THE SIGN OF THE SON OF MAN IN HEAVEN . . . AND THEY SHALL SEE THE SON OF MAN COMING IN POWER . . . THEN SHALL

TWO BE IN THE FIELD; THE ONE SHALL BE TAKEN, AND THE OTHER LEFT".

The only coming Christ teaches will take place is His "coming in power and great glory". At this coming, among other things to transpire, will be the visiting of retribution upon the unrighteous and the rewarding of the righteous.

Jesus is very careful to teach that His coming in power and great glory, and His coming as a bridegroom occur at one and the same time. The event occurs at midnight. Midnight is a point in time. It comes when the hour hand, the minute hand and the second hand stand right straight up on the clock dial and when the hour of twelve strikes. It is the specific point that marks the end of an old day and the beginning of the new. The bridegroom comes as the closing hour of the age strikes. His coming marks the opening of the new age. What could be clearer? Why read into the plain words of Jesus a meaning entirely foreign and false? There is no secret coming, nor any secret rapture in the teaching of Jesus. *"Let no man deceive you"*.

CHAPTER TWELVE
"The Escape Element In the Gospel"

The record of our Lord's Olivetic discourse as given in Luke, chapter 21, contains some very lucid statements regarding the return of Christ in relation to the Church. Striking phenomena will occur in the end of the age. Tribulation terrors will prevail. Believers are adjured, "Be not terrified". Verse 9. The exhortation is timely. There will be occasion for natural terror. "And great earthquakes shall be in divers places, and famine and pestilence; and fearful sights and great signs shall be from heaven." "Great earthquakes" and other extraordinary disturbances in the earth and in the atmospheric and the astronomical heavens are due to occur characterizing the Day of the Lord "Immediately after the tribulation". Beginning in the Tribulation, they climax in the Day of the Lord. Revelation 6:12; 8:5; 11:19; 16:18. They will come in the nature of a punishment upon the wicked and especially for their persecution of the saints during the Tribulation. Revelation 12:17; 13:7. "But before all these, they shall lay hands on you, and persecute you, delivering you up to the synagogues, and into prisons ... And there shall be signs in the sun, and in the moon, and in the stars; and upon the earth distress of nations with perplexity; the sea and the waves roaring . . . And WHEN these things begin to come to pass THEN look up, and lift up your heads; for your redemption draweth nigh". 11-28. Observe carefully that "WHEN" these things begin "THEN" redemption *draweth nigh*. It has not been realized yet — but it is approaching. This alone should suffice to rule out the hope of a

Pre-tribulation Rapture. The deliverance is to come *after the Tribulation is over*. It is near but not present.

Because the redemption has not yet been achieved, Jesus adds the exhortation: "Take heed to yourselves, . . . Watch ye therefore, and pray always, that ye may be accounted worthy to escape all these things that shall come to pass and to stand before the Son of man". 34, 36. The promise of "escape" is urged. The possibility of "escape" is assured, but conditioned upon one's willingness to "Watch . . . and pray always". Evidently, with this exhortation of Jesus in mind, Paul urges the Church, during the Tribulation, to watch for the Day of the Lord, and Christ's coming. 1 Thes. 5: 1-4. The desire to "escape" the terrors of the Great Tribulation is present with us. It is perfectly normal. We naturally shrink from suffering. It is a legitimate urge. However, granting all this, isn't there the temptation to "read into" this promise of Christ's, something He never meant to convey? There is no justification for supposing the escape-avenue will be by the Rapture route, before the Great Tribulation, or at any time during the days of it, terrible though it may become. This is not in the words of our text or their apparent sense. The esteemed, and able editor of a religious weekly recently wrote some words in another matter that might well be quoted in this connection because they express the thing I have in mind. The observations are built about what he referred to as "undue emphasis upon the escape element in the gospel". Anent this, he said: "The preacher is likely to make much of it, and to present it over and over again, returning to it night after night, supporting it with touching stories and pointing everything up to the happy moment when the reprieve is granted. The escape element is so glorious that it tends to become the beginning and the end of many persons' experience". How true! And what is true in this matter of personal salvation, is quite as true with reference to our longing for escape from the admitted "sorrows" of the Great Tribulation — and escape by being removed from the midst of them by what is aptly referred to as the Rapture.

Escape By Survival

Evidently such a hope is not predicated upon Scripture. It is not encouraged by God's Word. "Escape", yes — blessed escape. Always and properly, we may expect "escape". As in the case of Israel in Egypt, "escape" during the Tribulation will be by survival; "escape" at the conclusion of it will be by removal. "Escape" by survival has always been achieved in unfavorable predicaments in Scripture incidents, if the Bible records are reliable — and they are. The simple expedient of consulting a concordance will suffice to show that this escape-by-survival principle is prominent in some promises and some passages of the Bible. John 17: 15 shows it: "I pray not that Thou shouldest take them out of the world, but that Thou shouldest keep them from the evil". Likewise 1 Corinthians 10: 13 proves it: "God is faithful, Who will not suffer you to be tempted above that ye are able; but will with the temptation also make a way to escape, *that ye may be able to bear it*".

The Dragon And The Sun-Clothed Woman

The Revelation is a book of wonders. Some of the wonders are its parallelisms. For instance, there are two women pictured in it. A woman in Bible symbolism represents ecclesiasticism. A virtuous woman stands for the true Church, and a harlot woman represents false religion. In chapter seventeen of The

Revelation, John portrays a woman described as "the great whore" and "THE MOTHER OF HARLOTS". It is generally agreed among orthodox Bible teachers that this woman is a symbol of a system of apostate Christendom. This woman exists during a part of the Great Tribulation in a place called "the wilderness" sitting "upon a scarlet colored beast". Verse 3. The beast symbolizes Antichrist's ten-kingdom confederacy. Verses 12, 13. In chapter thirteen, verse fifteen, John says of the beast, "power was given unto him to continue for forty and two months"; or three years and a half. The woman is located in "the wilderness". In this place, which must be on the earth, she is to be utterly destroyed, for John declares: "The ten horns which thou sawest, and the beast, these shall hate the harlot, and shall make her desolate and naked, and shall eat her flesh, and shall burn her with fire." Verse 16. R.V.

In chapter twelve, John pictures a woman who is the very antithesis of the one in chapter seventeen. She is glorious in her purity. As a matter of logic, and correct interpretation of Bible symbols this woman can only represent the true Church. John says she is "clothed with the sun". Christ is described in Malachi 4:2 as "the Sun of Righteousness". To the Galatian believers Paul said: "As many of you as have been baptized into Christ have put on Christ." Galatians 3:27. Here, then, are those who have "put on Christ". They must be saved people; for only Christians "put on" Christ. The nations have never received Him. Israel has put Him off, for the time being, at least. Moreover, this "woman clothed with the sun" also has "the moon under her feet". Verse 1. The moon represents the law. Just as the moon reflects the light of the sun, so the law reflects the righteousness of Christ. The unregenerate Gentiles are without grace, and disobedient Israel is "under the law". However, Christians are above the law. The Church stands in victory with the law "under her feet". Other things are said about this woman to support the claim that she symbolizes the true Church. However, my purpose here is not to give an exhaustive exposition of the symbol, as helpful as it might prove to be to some readers. I merely point out the fact that this "woman", like the "harlot woman", will also be on earth. Both are in "the wilderness" at the same time. Unlike the "whore", who perishes as the victim of the beast's hate, the "woman clothed with the Sun [of Righteousness]" is preserved, being the object of Christ's affection, the recipient of His power. How could John make all these facts clearer than he did in the plain language he used in Revelation 12:6?: "And the woman fled *into the wilderness*, where she hath a place prepared of God, *that they should feed her there a thousand two hundred and three score days.*"

The harlot woman is in the wilderness during a part of the forty and two months, or three years and a half of the Great Tribulation. The Sun-clad woman is there during that entire period. I resort to repetition for the sake of emphasis. These facts seem so very relevant and important because they deal a death blow to Pre-tribulation-rapturism by showing the Church (symbolized by the Sun-clad woman) to be on earth during the reign of the Antichrist and throughout the period of the Great Tribulation. We observe that the woman is "fed" and "nourished" during the Tribulation under the Antichrist, even as Elijah, the "an hundred prophets", and the remainder of the "seven thousand" faithful people of God, were fed and nourished during the typical tribulation under wicked Ahab, 1 Kings 17:1-16; 18:1-13; 19:18, who is a striking type of the Antichrist. John said: "And to the woman were given two wings of a great eagle, that she might fly into the wilderness, into her place, where she is nourished for a time [one year], and times [two years], and half a time [half a year]". Verse 14. Satanic hate and hellish forces are directed against the woman in a diabolical effort to destroy her: "And the serpent cast out of his mouth water as a flood after the woman, that he might cause her to be carried away of the flood". Revelation 12:15. The record clearly states that the woman, representing the true Church, is "nourished" during the Tribulation, and thus neither Satan nor Antichrist can prevail against her. Christ declared: "I will build My Church; and the gates of hell shall not prevail against it". Matt. 16:18. Christ's promises are as valid and His power as victorious for Tribulation days as for pre-tribulation times. I say very freely that Pre-tribulation-rapturism cannot stand before such clear facts as presented by the Sun-clad woman in The Revelation. Could it be that Solomon was previewing this scene? He asked: "Who is this that *cometh up from the wilderness,* leaning upon her beloved?". Song of Solomon 8:5. If so, then he too was teaching what all other Bible penmen have taught, that the Church will be *"caught up to meet the Lord"* as she *"cometh up from the wilderness, leaning upon her beloved" "immediately after the tribulation".* This is all so very clear, that *only those who will not receive it cannot see it!*

Shipwrecked — But Escaped

A graphic description of a shipwreck is found in Acts 27. Paul and two hundred and seventy-five other persons were on board. The vessel floundered and was totally destroyed by the storm that swept the sea. The apostle had been given the assurance from God that although the ship would be demolished by the fury of the sea, there would be no loss of life. The narrative closes with the significant sentence: "And it came to pass that they all ESCAPED safe to land". Acts 27: 44. How did they ESCAPE? The answer is divinely given — they survived the fury of the storm by being kept in it. The ship was utterly demolished. All were precipitated into the treacherous waters. They all ESCAPED. Saints, likewise, may "escape safe" in the coming Great Tribulation storm.

Escaping Corruption

Less dramatic than the story of the Dragon and the Sun-clad woman; or Luke's shipwreck narrative, and the survival of the total passenger list, is the assurance given by Peter when he said: "Having ESCAPED the corruption that is in the world through lust". 2 Peter 1: 4. Nonetheless is it true that the ESCAPE-SURVIVAL principle is set forth. Not only did believers in Peter's day escape corruption, although surrounded by it, but so do present-day saints. Human society is saturated with corruption, yet we "ESCAPE the corruption that is in the world through lust". How? You and I know the answer, but let Peter tell it by inspired words: *"Kept by the power of God through faith unto salvation ready to be revealed in the last time".* 1 Peter 1: 5.

God's ESCAPE-SURVIVAL principle is beautifully told in an inspiring episode from China's modern night of terror. I read this story as a part of my morning devotion period today, hence it is still fresh in my mind. J. B. Tweter narrates it. It is filled with tears.

It evokes praise to God — the God Who keeps in the midst of trial. Bandits swooped down upon Shansi, China, on a fateful night in June, 1920. "One lone lady missionary within the village kept a mission school for about forty girls. How was she to keep them safe from the hands of these lawless men from the hills? . . . She called all of the girls together into the classroom, explained their danger and calmly asked them all to kneel and commit themselves into the care of their Almighty God.

" 'Oh, God, our heavenly Father', the missionary prayed, 'we have no might but in Thee. Please send some guardian angel to protect us this night'. . . . Toward morning all sounds died down to a whisper. The bandits had overrun all the village, accomplished all their desires, then stole away again at dawn to their secret haunts in the hills. Not one had attempted to enter the school compound with the forty girls sheltered within. . . . Dead bodies lay in the streets, or astride open doorways. Young girls were weeping in the arms of their mothers. . . . 'God in His mercy spared us and our school of girls', said the missionary.

" 'No wonder!' the villagers replied with awe. 'The bandits did not dare molest you. On each corner of your compound wall — standing on guard — we saw four angels with drawn swords in their hands' ". ESCAPE by SURVIVAL not by REMOVAL. "Pray always, that ye may be accounted worthy to *escape*", by being kept in the midst of Tribulation.

CHAPTER THIRTEEN
Two Resurrections — One Rapture

The future resurrection of the dead is amply assured both as a matter of divine revelation and human reason. The clear teaching of the Word of God is that dead bodies will be raised. In words as clear as words can possibly be, Scripture informs us that there will be two resurrections. That is, resurrections that differ in respect to the time they take place and also regarding those who will participate. Let us first of all give the Scripture reference: "There shall be a resurrection of the dead, both of the just and unjust". Acts 24:15. "Marvel not at this: for the hour is coming, in the which all that are in the graves shall hear His voice, and shall come forth; they that have done good, unto the resurrection of life; and they that have done evil, unto the resurrection of damnation". John 5:28, 29.

The two resurrections will be separated by a thousand years. The righteous dead will be resurrected at the time of the Lord's return: "For the Lord Himself shall descend from heaven . . . and the dead in Christ shall rise". 1 Thessalonians 4:16. "Blessed and holy is he that hath part in the first resurrection." Revelation 20:6. The "unjust" dead are to be resurrected following an interval of one thousand years: "The rest of the [unjustified] dead lived not again until the thousand years were finished". Revelation 20:5. We desire only honest exegesis of Scripture. Let us shun any tendency to "read into" the Bible something that is not there. There are to be two future resurrections — no more. Any more than two must be conjured as an expedient to bolster a false notion of Scripture. Just two, mind

you, and no more. God says two — and let God be
true! Romans 3:4.

"At the Last Day"

As the thought of the resurrection came into view
here, I found my mind reverting to chapter six and
eleven of John's gospel. In turning to these chapters
in my Bible I discovered that at sometime in the past
I had underscored a number of verses. Jesus is preaching His sermon on the Bread of Life. He says: "Of all
which He hath given Me I should lose nothing, but
should raise it up again at *the last day* . . . everyone
which . . . believeth on Him . . . I will raise him up at
the last day. . . . No man can come to Me except the
Father . . . draw him: and I will raise him up at *the
last day.* . . . whoso eateth My flesh, and, drinketh My
blood, hath eternal life; and I will raise him up at
the last day". John 6:39, 40, 44, 54. These definite statements permit of no quibbling. We take them at their
face value. The saints are to be resurrected "at the
last day". Not a day before "the last day" of the age.
Let "the last day" mean just that. Don't "read into"
these statements anything about any period of time
before "the last day".

Had Jesus not meant what He had previously declared, the death of Lazarus would have presented Him
with an excellent opportunity to make the correction.
Instead, however, He uses it as an occasion to give
emphasis to this fact. Said the bereaved Martha: "I
know that he shall rise again in *the resurrection at
the last day*". John 11:24. This is the verification of His
own teaching — *"at the last day"*.

"The Last Trump"

"The last" must convey the thought of finality —
nothing beyond it — "the last". This is the meaning it

has when Paul testifies: "And *last of all* He was seen of me". It is certainly the meaning when he goes on to assert: *"The last enemy* that shall be destroyed is death". We know there were but two Adams, the first and the last, hence it has the meaning of finality when the apostle writes: *"The last Adam* was made a quickening spirit". The principle proves to be a preface to the teaching of Paul that the rapture and the resurrection of all saints will take place at *the last trump.* Here are his words: "Behold I show you a mystery; we shall not all sleep, but we shall all be changed in a moment, in the twinkling of an eye, *at the last trump*: for the trumpet shall sound, and the dead shall be raised incorruptible, and we shall be changed". 1 Corinthians 15: 8, 26, 45, 51, 52. We observe two facts. First, ALL are to be resurrected and renovated simultaneously. Second, this will take place at the LAST trumpet. The only trumpets to sound, that appear in the New Testament, are those that are heard in connection with the Great Tribulation, and the return of Christ. A series of seven trumpets are sounded. As the LAST is blown, the Tribulation ends, and voices announce the coming of the Lord to establish His kingdom: "And the seventh angel sounded; and there were great voices in heaven, saying, The kingdoms of this world are become the kingdoms of our Lord, and of His Christ; and He shall reign for ever and ever". Revelation 11: 15. This should settle the issue. *At the end of the age — on the last day, Christ will come to resurrect and rapture His saints.*

"There Will The Rapture Be Also"

It is such an obvious fact. The truth has been so eloquently phrased by Alexander Reese: "Where the resurrection is, there will the rapture be also". Any student of the Bible will readily admit that there are clear, plain, straight - forward statements of a coming Rapture to be found in the Word of God. It is a blessed truth. The soul thrills at the prospect of such a glorious event. It reacts like martial music upon the souls of saints. We would not risk minimizing the glory of it in any way. However, I do feel that we may have been emphasizing it out of all proportion to its *comparative* importance in the second coming program.

In Matthew 24:31 Christ strongly declares the Rapture of the Church. In this Thessalonian epistle Paul enlarges upon that statement and makes a positive assertion that it will take place. This letter was not written by Paul primarily to teach the Rapture of the Church, much less was it intended to convey the idea that the Rapture would come before the Tribulation. In chapter four the Rapture is taught — this we grant and gladly. However, it is but an incident referred to by Paul to correct an error that had become quite prevalent among the saints. Nothing is said in this chapter of the time of the Rapture. However in the first four verses of the next chapter, Paul shows when it will occur, for he says: "But of the times and the seasons, brethren, ye have no need that I write unto you. For yourselves know perfectly that the day of the Lord so cometh as a thief in the night. For when they shall say, Peace and safety; then sudden destruction cometh upon them, as travail upon a woman with child; and they shall not escape. But ye, brethren, are not in darkness, that that day should overtake you as a thief". Thus in this epistle he repeats to these Thessalonians what he had told them when he was with them, that the time of the Rapture will be the Day of the Lord, and so fully agreeing with the Lord, from

Whose "word", or statement, he was quoting, that it
will take place "immediately after the tribulation". If
Paul had supposed that the Church is to be raptured
before the Tribulation, he could and probably would,
when referring to the Day of the Lord, have said: "That
day shall not overtake you", but he would not have
added, "as a thief", as he does: for that addition is a
clear intimation, which is in harmony with the rest
of those four verses, that there will be a great danger
of its doing so, unless they are watchful. Perhaps it
is because of this that some Pre-tribulation-rapturists,
who venture to quote these four verses, which few of
them do, omit these three words: "as a thief". When
the division of Scripture into chapters and verses took
place, it resulted, in some instances, in careless and un-
fortunate division. Here is a case in point. The final
four verses of chapter four rightly belong at the beginning of chapter five. Leave them where they are
and their meaning is largely concealed. Put them
where they should logically be and the meaning is
clear — *the Rapture is to take place on the Day of the
Lord.*

During his extensive missionary travels, Paul had
journeyed to Thessalonica. There he ministered the
Word of God: "And Paul, as his manner was, went in
unto them, and three sabbath days reasoned with them
out of the Scriptures. . . . And some of them [Jews]
believed, . . . And of the devout Greeks a great multitude, and of the chief women not a few". Acts 17:1-4.
On this teaching mission the Apostle had taught these
Thessalonian believers the essential and vital doctrines
concerning Christ and the Christian faith, and stress
had been placed upon the promised return of Christ,
and related events. 2 Thes. 2:5. Following Paul's de-
parture, perhaps because of a dearth of Spirit-taught

teachers, error crept in. Truth was perverted. Facts were beclouded. Saints were bewildered and discouraged. Notice of this came to Paul. He wrote an epistle to these Thessalonian Christians. In it he sought to confirm the truths already taught to them and thus to establish them in the Word of God. The second coming of Christ is prominent in the epistle because the apostle undertakes to refute a false teaching regarding Christ's return and thus to comfort the deceived and disheartened disciples. Great grief had been caused by the erroneous teaching that "sleeping" saints, because of their untimely death, would not be privileged to behold Christ's coming. Departed believers would remain in the grave and so would not experience the joy of the fulfilment of Christ's promise. He had said: "I will come again, and receive you unto Myself, that where I am, there ye may be also". John 14: 3. Hence, an epistle is sent to these mistaught Christians. In the letter Paul corrects the error in teaching, and attempts to comfort his "brethren" with the truth that death will in no way rob Christians of their redemption-right to participate in the glory of Christ's return. Death will not give living saints an advantage, by permitting them, alone, to welcome the returning Redeemer, so that only they will be with Him. The truth is, says the apostle, the dead in Christ will first be resurrected, and then, together with the living saints, they will be "caught up to meet" their returning Lord.

It might be helpful at this point just to read what Paul actually wrote: "But I would not have you to be ignorant, brethren, concerning them which are asleep, that ye sorrow not, even as others which have no hope. For if we believe that Jesus died and rose again, even so them also which sleep, in Jesus will God bring with Him. For this we say unto you by the word of the Lord, that we which are alive and remain unto the coming of the Lord shall not prevent them which are asleep. For the Lord Himself shall descend from heaven with a shout, with the voice of the arch-angel, and with the trump of God; and the dead in Christ shall rise first: then we which are alive and remain shall be caught up together with them in the clouds, to meet the Lord in the air; and so shall we ever be with the Lord. Wherefore comfort one another with these words". 1 Thessalonians 4: 13-18. It will be seen from this passage, and the situation that caused the writing of it, that the teaching about the Rapture here is incidental. Resurrection is primary — Rapture is secondary: *"The dead in Christ shall rise first"* — that's the crux of the corrective teaching. "Then we which are alive and remain shall be caught up together with them in the clouds, to meet the Lord in the air" — that's the corollary of the corrective statement.

"Overtake You As A Thief"

In this corrective teaching, Paul makes not the faintest suggestion that this resurrection and the ac-companying rapture will take place before the Great Tribulation. Fortunately, for those who want to know the truth about the time of the resurrection and rap-ture of the saints, the time element was included in Paul's teaching here. By word of mouth Paul had in-structed these Thessalonian Christians regarding "the coming of our Lord Jesus Christ, and our gathering together unto Him". He had taught them about the Apostasy, and the Tribulation, and the coming of the Man of Sin, as he later wrote and reminded them, saying: "Remember ye not, that, when I was yet with you, I told you these things". 2 Thessalonians 2: 5.

Paul had given forth previous teaching about the Rapture; but he had made no promise of saints escaping the Great Tribulation by being raptured before it.

Contrary to popular theory of a Pre-tribulation Rapture the inspired apostle proceeds in his letter to assure the Christians that they would know when to look for the return of their Lord, "For yourselves know perfectly that the day of the Lord so cometh *as a thief in the night*. For when *they* shall say, Peace and safety: then sudden destruction cometh upon *them*, as travail upon a woman with child; and *they* shall not escape. But *ye,* brethren, are not in darkness, that that day should overtake *you as a thief*". 1 Thessalonians 5: 2-4. He gave them no assurance it would *not overtake them*. He pointed out that it *would overtake saint and sinner without discrimination.* However, it will overtake sinners "as a thief", because they will not have believed previous warnings. It will overtake you — make no mistake as to that, said Paul — but *not as a thief.* You will be prepared for this eventuality because you will have heeded the Word of God.

It is significant, and true, because our Lord says so, that He will "come as a thief"; but where saints are concerned this need not be the case, because of prior warning. Christ is addressing His Church in Revelation 16: 15 when He adds, as He tells of gathering the whole world to Armageddon, the battle of that great day of God Almighty, "Behold, I come as a thief. Blessed is he that watcheth, and keepeth his garments, lest he walk naked, and they see his shame". It is also true, because very clearly told by Jesus and Paul, that Christ will "come as a thief" to the unsaved involved, because a lack of spiritual understanding has kept them from making proper preparation. In warning His disciples and the unbelievers of His return, Jesus said:

"And take heed to *yourselves* [His disciples] lest at any time *your* hearts be overcharged with surfeiting and drunkenness, and cares of this life, and so THAT DAY come upon *you* unawares. *For as a snare shall it come upon all them that dwell upon the face of the whole earth.* Watch *ye* therefore and pray always that *ye* may be accounted worthy to escape all these things that shall come to pass, and to stand before the Son of Man". Luke 21: 34-36. "That day" will "come upon" all of you — don't be misled about that. However, if *you* "take heed" and "watch", it will not come upon *you* "as a snare". *You* can "escape" by being "kept by the power of God through faith" even in the midst of the awful scenes of that day.

Writing of that same "day" and of the same events, and to the same two classes of people involved, Paul says the same things, for the same purpose: "But of the times and seasons *brethren, ye* have no need that I write unto *you.* For *yourselves* know perfectly that the day of the Lord so cometh *as a thief* in the night. For when *they* [the unsaved] shall say, Peace and safety; then sudden destruction cometh upon *them,* as travail upon a woman with child; and *they shall not escape.* But *ye brethren* are not in darkness, [unless you believe in Pre-tribulation-rapturism] that THAT DAY should overtake *you* as a thief. . . . Therefore let *us* not sleep, as do *others;* but let *us* watch and be sober". 1 Thessalonians 5: 2: 6.

Now, very kindly, and seriously, and prayerfully, I ask you, beloved reader: Would you hear and heed and be helped by these Holy Spirit inspired words and warnings regarding the Post-tribulation coming of Christ? Or, would you rather believe and thus be deceived and hindered by the Satan inspired teaching of a Pre-tribulation return of Christ given first to Margaret Macdonald and propagated subsequently by others? We can safely believe anything taught by the Godhead. Jesus said, "I am the truth". Christ declared of the Holy Spirit, "He will guide you into all truth". Of men we cannot be so sure. Of some of them Job said, "But ye are forgers of lies". Job 13:4.

Two resurrections — one rapture. To teach more is to contend for something unscriptural. In Paul's direct reference to the Rapture in 1 Thessalonians, the resurrection of the saints and the coming of the Lord are accompanying events. Suppose the Lord should rapture His saints before, or even during the Great Tribulation, then it would be necessary to repeat the resurrection and the rapture when He comes again to accommodate those who will have been saved during the Tribulation. The bodies of those who will die from martyrdom, or from natural causes, during the reign of Antichrist cannot be left in their graves. Therefore, the Pre-tribulation-rapture fallacy requires man to arrange for an extra resurrection and an additional rapture. Again the words of Revelation 20:5, 6 come to mind. They tell of two resurrections: one of the just, another of the unjust. The words of Revelation 22:18 again come before me: "If any man shall add unto these things, God shall add unto him the plagues that are written in this book". Even if we be charitable and agree that the Lord has in mind a wilful, deliberate act of adding, it still remains a serious offense. Can one afford to risk being guilty? Must we "add" more resurrections and raptures than those arranged by God? We must, if the Pre-tribulation-resurrection-rapture teaching is fact and not fancy.

Vindication of Humiliation

Perhaps, in our zeal for truth, and enthusiasm to propagate the good news of Christ's second advent, we may have lost sight of the primary purpose of His coming. Primarily, it will be the vindication of His humiliation. The incarnation must justly be followed by the exaltation. "He humbled Himself, and became obedient unto death, even the death of the cross. Wherefore God hath also highly exalted Him . . . that . . . every knee should bow . . . and that every tongue should confess that Jesus Christ is Lord." Philippians 2:8-11.

In His first advent, Jesus was encouraged to perfect obedience to the Father and complete fidelity to His redemptive mission, by a promise from His Father. It was the promise of reward. He was inspired by a perfectly legitimate motive — the reward motive. So we are told in Hebrews 12:2: "Who for the *joy* that was set before Him endured the cross". This "joy" of earned reward is very clearly told in Psalm 2:8, 9: "Ask of Me and I shall give Thee the heathen [nations] for Thine inheritance, and the uttermost parts of the earth for Thy possession. Thou shalt break them with a rod of iron; Thou shalt dash them in pieces like a potter's vessel". To realize this reward He will return.

All other events related to His return — and they are numerous — are vital, but merely incidental and complementary. The one overwhelming purpose will be to possess in power the kingdom He has won by His patience and perseverance. We should avoid the temptation of yielding to the tendency to stress other considerations out of proportion to this all-important purpose. When, by unwarranted emphasis we make the Rapture of saints the focal point of prophecy, we wrongfully — even if unwittingly — project ourselves into the picture, and thus crowd Him out to a great extent. Must we, by selfishly stressing our humble participation in the program, overshadow Him and ob-

scure the purpose of His advent in glory? It is HIS
coming. It is HIS crowning glory. It is HIS promised
reward. HE is to benefit primarily. HE will be the
"leading actor" in the drama of the second coming.
The saints will be but "bit players". One gets the im-
pression, from the over-emphasis upon the Rapture,
that men are trying to "steal the show". It is HIS
"curtain call". We should be content, as the "supporting cast", to remain in "the wings" and rejoice that He
has triumphed and is being honored. The spotlight in
the transfiguration scene fell upon Jesus. The saints
who accompanied Him did not occupy the center of
the stage. The pageant of the triumphal entry points
up the fact that HE was the center of attraction. No
man sought to turn the acclaim of the multitudes to
himself: "The whole multitude of the disciples began
to rejoice and praise God with a loud voice for all the
mighty works which they had seen; saying, Blessed
be the king". Luke 19: 37, 38.

CHAPTER FOURTEEN
"The Full End of the Age"

It is impossible to think without distinctions. We live in a world of opposites. Truth conflicts with error. Good is opposed to bad. Righteousness and sin are deadly enemies. The law of opposites prevails. According to this law, distinctions are made, so we are one thing, or we are something else. We are Christians or we are not Christians. We are saved or we are not saved. The logic of the law of opposites leads us to believe there is a hell and a heaven. Reason says there must be a reward for goodness and retribution for wickedness.

The Master in His early teaching by employing parables, clarified the matter and divided the human family into two distinct groups — saved and lost. If there are two classes, saved and lost, then there are two destinies. This, Jesus taught. Among other symbols used by Jesus, He likens the saved to "wheat" and the lost to "tares". "The good seed are the children of the kingdom; but the tares are the children of the wicked one; the enemy that sowed them is the devil; the harvest is the end of the world [age]." Matthew 13:38, 39. Now, the significant fact is, that the Saviour assures us there will be no gathering out of the "wheat", or saved, from among the "tares", or lost, until the *full end of the age.* His followers might wish it otherwise, but the matter is settled once for all by Jesus. "The servants said unto Him, Wilt Thou then that we go and gather them up? But He said, Nay; . . . *let both grow together until the harvest;* and in the time of

harvest I will say to the reapers, Gather together *first
the tares,* and bind them in bundles to burn them;
but gather the wheat into My barn." Matthew 13: 28-30.
There is no Pre-tribulation-rapture teaching here —
"Let both grow together until the harvest". When will
the harvest be? *"The harvest is the end of the world*
[*age*]*."* When, therefore, the tares are gathered and
burned in the fire; and the wheat is gathered and stored
in His barn — *"the end of this world* [*age*]*",* Matthew
13: 39, 40, will have come.

By consulting Young's Concordance (I mention this
that any reader may verify) I note that the word "consummation" as used in the Revised Version and the
word "end" employed in the Authorized Version, is
a translation from the word "sunteleia" and is used
in six instances in the New Testament. The literal
meaning of the word "sunteleia" is given as *"full end".*
Of the six usages, five are found in Matthew's gospel
and are definitely used with reference to Christ's return. Observe then what the word reveals concerning
the time of Christ's coming and the separation of saints
from sinners for the purpose of rewarding the one and
punishing the other:

"The harvest is the *full end of the age."* Matthew
13: 39;

"So shall it be in the *full end of the age."* Matthew
13: 40;

"So shall it be in the *full end of the age."* Matthew
13: 49.

The revelation of Christ; the rapture and rewarding
of His Church; and the retribution of the wicked are
all placed at the *"full end of the age".* The disciples
may have been "slow of heart to believe all that the
prophets have spoken" but they evidently understood
enough to cause them to enquire "What shall be the

sign of Thy coming and of the SUNTELEIA [*full end*] *of the world* [*age*]?". Matthew 24:3. They knew of no coming before *"the full end of the age"*; and for good reason — there will be none.

The Lord's prayer is more than a prayer. It incorporates some blessed and vital gospel truths. The coming of the King to establish His kingdom of power and glory is among them. No hint is given, however, of a Pre-tribulation coming. If there is to be, could we not expect at least some slight hint of it? Some statement — any word — would tend to make it authentic. The idea would be lifted out of the realm of the speculative and hypothetical. A rare opportunity of making a Pre-tribulation-rapture statement was afforded when Jesus commissioned His disciples to be world-evangelizers and added the comforting assurance of His presence while they evangelized. He offered no reason for supposing that His presence would be needed only until some years before the close of the age, by reason of a rapture then taking place. What He did say exactly is: "Lo, I am with you alway, even unto *the* [*full*] *end of the world* [*age*]". Matthew 28:20.

"Waiting For The Revelation"

While many teach the Rapture before the Tribulation, they would also agree that the revelation of Christ will occur at the end of the Tribulation. Paul found occasion to thank the Lord for the "Church of God which is at Corinth". Then he commends them for their faith, evidenced in a number of ways: "So that ye come behind in no gift; waiting for the coming [Greek, *'apocalypse', revelation*] of our Lord Jesus Christ: Who shall also confirm you [make you steadfast] unto the end [*until the full end*], that ye may be blameless in the day of our Lord Jesus Christ". 1 Corinthians 1: 4-8. What were the saints "waiting for"? The Rapture before the Tribulation? No! They were "waiting for the revelation of our Lord Jesus Christ"; and, said Paul, that same Lord would "make them steadfast unto *the full end of the age*".

Grace And Joy At The Revelation

Peter received a three-fold commission from his Master. First, the big fisherman was to become a great manfisher. Second, he was to "strengthen the brethren". Third, he was to "feed My sheep". Two epistles were written in an endeavor to fulfil these commissions. He strengthens, or encourages, the brethren by assuring them "that the trial of your faith, being much more precious than of gold that perisheth, though it be tried with fire, might be found unto praise and honour and glory at the appearing [Greek, *'apocalypse', revelation*] of Jesus Christ. . . . Wherefore gird up the loins of your mind, be sober, and hope to *the end* [*full end*] for the grace that is to be brought unto you at the *revelation of Jesus Christ*". 1 Peter 1: 7-13. The grace and joy of the Church are to become hers when the Lord comes in glory. The Church is told to hope for *the full end of the age*, when her Lord is to be revealed. What becomes of the present-day teaching that urges saints to hope for His coming to rapture them perhaps seven years or at some period prior to the full end of the age and the revelation of Christ? Scripture utterly rules it out!

Does the faithful apostle in his endeavor to strengthen God's people, hold out the false hope of escaping the Tribulation by rapture? Not at all. He encourages by assurance of survival, rather than removal. "Beloved, *think it not strange concerning the fiery trial that is to try you, as though some strange thing hap-*

pened unto you: but rejoice, inasmuch as ye are partakers of Christ's sufferings; that, *when His glory shall
be revealed,* ye may be glad also with exceeding joy.
. . . If any man suffer as a Christian let him not be
ashamed; but let him glorify God on this behalf."
1 Peter 4: 12-16. The fiery trial of present tribulation may try Christians, says Peter; but they will
ultimately be vindicated. The apostle admonishes
suffering saints and assures them that it will not be
all loss to suffer for Christ's sake. If they endure
these trials, they will rejoice that they did so, when
the Lord returns. Said he, *"When He shall be revealed
in His glory"* they shall "be glad with exceeding joy"
because *then their deliverance will come.* When will
these saints, who, as "partakers of Christ's sufferings
[or sufferings for Christ]" have endured "fiery trial",
rejoice in deliverance and reward? — *"When He shall
be revealed in His glory."* There is no Pre-tribulation-
rapture in Peter's preaching.

Recompensed At The Close Of The Tribulation

Paul had felt the heavy hand of trouble. He had felt
the bitter lash and sting of suffering as few had, for he
was "in labours [hardships] more abundant, in stripes
above measure, in prisons more frequent, in deaths oft".
2 Corinthians 11: 23. He knew that in justice to himself,
there would come a time of reckoning; that he would
be recompensed for his trials, and his persecutors and
tormentors would be justly and drastically dealt with
and punished. With this confidence he continued on
his pilgrim way and preached to his fellow-sufferers.
Hence he writes to the Thessalonians: "Which is a
manifest token of the righteous judgment of God, that
ye may be counted worthy of the kingdom of God, *for
which ye also suffer;* seeing it is a righteous thing with

God to recompense tribulation to them that trouble you; and to you who are troubled rest with us, *when the Lord Jesus shall be revealed from heaven with His mighty angels, . . . When He shall come to be glorified in His saints*, and to be admired in [Greek, 'en' — by] all them that believe [because our testimony among you was believed] in that day". 2 Thessalonians 1: 5-10.

In substance Paul says: If you are being persecuted by the wicked, be patient. Rest assured with me, that you may expect nothing else, or better, from the ungodly. However, there will come a day of recompense "for ye which also suffer". Help will come. Deliverance is promised. It is coming "when the Lord Jesus shall be revealed from heaven with His mighty angels. . . . He shall be glorified in His saints". To expect to be delivered before "He shall come to be glorified in His saints" is to build on a false hope. Here, instead, Paul encourages troubled, or persecuted saints, by notifying them that God will surely do two things. 1) "Recompense tribulation to them that trouble [persecute] you." 2) "And to you who are troubled [persecuted] rest with us [who also are troubled or persecuted]." When will the righteous God "recompense" this "tribulation" to the persecutor; and this "rest" to the persecuted? We have the Spirit-inspired answer: "When the Lord shall be revealed from heaven with His mighty angels, in flaming fire taking vengeance on them that know not God". What! Paul, can't you tell us that we will escape the Tribulation by being raptured some time before "the Lord Jesus shall be revealed with His mighty angels, in flaming fire taking vengeance upon them that know not God"? No — that's out! It's not in the program! To teach you so would be to deceive you, and inspire you with a hope that will fail.

CHAPTER FIFTEEN
"Ye Shall Have Tribulation"

I sometimes think that some people become Christians laboring under a misapprehension. They think of the Christian life as a sort of charmed life. If they become Christians all their troubles will be ended or mended. Surely such souls soon have a rude awakening. Immunity from trouble has not been promised for being good or Godly. We love sunshine, but the Arabs have a saying, "All sunshine makes a desert". It is a matter of observation, that the graces of the Christian life are more apparent in the lives of those who have gone through tribulation. God wants to get as rich crops as possible from the soil of our lives. There are certain plants of the Christian life, such as humility, gentleness, meekness, which cannot come to perfection if the sun of prosperity be perpetually shining. Spurgeon said: "Suffering is the best piece of furniture in my home. All the grace I got out of my comfortable, easy time might almost lie on a penny. The good I have received from my trials, pains, and griefs, is incalculable. What I do owe to the fire and file, the crucible and the furnace, the bellows, and the hands that thrust me into the heat!".

The human spirit abhors suffering. We shrink from tribulation. It is no doubt this natural aversion to trial that has given the Pre-tribulation-rapture fallacy such a hold upon believers. It is no doubt one of the reasons for its popularity. "The wish is father to the thought." We want it so and accommodate our desire by spinning a web of theological fancy. But, can we trust a carnal, cowardly nature to plan a spiritual and chivalrous pro-

s? Would it not be better to let the all-wise
olent and beneficent God chart our course?

There is a word in frequent use in Scripture. In our
English version of the Bible this word, for the most
part, appears as "tribulation". In the Greek it is
"thlipsis". Some forty-four times at least, it is used.
In various forms it is found; always with the same
root meaning. A summary shows it is translated thus:
burdened 1, anguish 1, persecution 1, trouble 3, affliction 17, tribulation 21. A concordance, or help, can be
consulted to verify this claim.

Pre-tribulation-rapturists for the most part teach
that the righteous will be raptured before the Tribulation as reward for their faithfulness; the wicked are
to be left to face Tribulation because of their wickedness. It should at least deliver a heavy jolt — if not
a knock-out blow — to this theory to show that of the
forty-four times where the word "Tribulation" appears
in Scripture, in thirty-six instances it is employed to
teach us that tribulation is associated with Christians.
It will not be necessary to give all the references. A
few will suffice to support the claim: "In the world ye
shall have tribulation: but be of good cheer". John
16:33. "Fear none of these things which thou shalt
suffer: behold, the devil shall cast some of you into
prison, that ye may be tried; and ye shall have tribulation ten days; be thou faithful unto death, and I will
give thee a crown of life." Revelation 2:10. "We must
through much tribulation enter into the kingdom."
Acts 14:22. "And not only so, but we glory in tribulation also, knowing that tribulation worketh patience."
Romans 5:3. "For verily, when we were with you,
we told you before that we should suffer tribulation."
1 Thessalonians 3:4.

We must learn to distinguish between wrath and tribulation. *Wrath* is reserved for the unrepentant wicked. Tribulation is a possibility for the saint. "For God hath not appointed *us* to wrath." 1 Thessalonians 5: 9. If Scripture is true, then Christians may experience tribulation. Suffering purifies and perfects. If we understand the wholesome benefits and the divine purpose in tribulation, then we would realize that we can do without ease and comfort, but we cannot spare one trial or sorrow. Trial develops the spiritual nature. Therefore the greater the tribulation the greater the development. So it is not to be wondered at that during the Tribulation John "heard a voice from heaven saying unto him, Write, Blessed are the dead *which die in the Lord from henceforth*", and later is shown the Tribulation martyrs placed in the forefront of the first resurrection saints to receive special recognition.

If you are unable to harmonize tribulation with the logic of the Christian life, then behold your Lord — "A man of sorrows and acquainted with grief". Isaiah 53: 3. When He came into Mary's life, she too "became a [woman] of sorrows and acquainted with grief". "Yea, a sword shall pierce through thy own soul also." Luke 2: 35. Should we expect to be favored above our Lord and this choice saint? When He comes into our lives it may well be true of us: "In the world ye shall have tribulation". John 16: 33.

We could pile Scripture upon Scripture, but sufficient has been set down to convince anyone that tribulation may be the portion of Christians. Though this be true, none should shrink from it. None should cower at its approach, for just as sure as it is endured, it will result in eternal and substantial reward; a reward not to be spurned, but to be earnestly desired. "If we suffer [with Him] we shall also reign with Him." 2 Timothy 2:12. God is a consummate artist. He can take the salt of our tears; the blue of our bruises; the red of our blood, and paint pictures that will last for ever: "For our light affliction, which is but for a moment, worketh for us a far more exceeding, and eternal weight of glory". 2 Corinthians 4:17.

Oh, friends, shrink not from tribulation; but rather covet it, embrace it, wrap it about your souls as an armor of strength, and inspiration! Cleave to it as a talisman against slothfulness. "But the God of all grace, Who hath called us unto His eternal glory by Christ Jesus, after that ye have *suffered awhile* make you perfect, stablish, strengthen, settle you." 1 Peter 5:10.

CHAPTER SIXTEEN

"Behold, I Come As A Thief"

Prophecy is the mold of history. It presents the shape of things to come. It is history written beforehand. Prophecy is the divine record of events before they take place. The divinely inspired teaching of future things is important. Eschatology is a vital part of the Gospel. The Bible shows a progressive development. It moves inexorably from the glory of creation in the divine declaration: "In the beginning God created the heaven and the earth", on to the triumphal theme, "And I saw a new heaven and a new earth; for the first heaven and the first earth were passed away; . . . Behold I make all things new". Genesis 1:1; Revelation 21:1, 5. It is in keeping with the coherency of Scripture that The Revelation should give a clear, comprehensive schedule of "the things which shall be hereafter". It is a Book of Consummations. Events that close this age are set forth. The "last days" are graphically described. It is a Book of Coronation. Christ returns. The King is crowned. He ascends His throne. He assumes His divine prerogatives. He reigns and rules with power and authority. "Behold, He cometh with clouds; and every eye shall see Him." "To Him be glory and dominion for ever and ever. Amen." "For He is Lord of lords, and King of kings." "And He hath on His vesture and on His thigh a name written, KING OF KINGS, AND LORD OF LORDS." "Amen. Even so, come, Lord Jesus." Revelation 1:6, 7; 17:14; 22:20.

No Pre-Tribulation-Rapture Of The Church In The Revelation

Inasmuch as the second coming and related events are clearly presented in The Revelation, one would suppose that if the Rapture is an important feature of the coming it would have been told in this Book. But, quite to the contrary, it is nowhere specifically presented as a part of the second coming program. There is no direct teaching regarding the Rapture of the Church. Certainly there is not so much as the slightest hint of a *Pre-tribulation-rapture for the Church*. A rapture, in the more specific sense of a translation, is pictured in The Revelation. There are at least two cases involving translation to heaven during the latter times. The Sun-clad woman gives birth to a child. Satan desires to "devour" her offspring at its birth. He is prevented from doing so, being frustrated by the translation of the child to heaven: "And she brought forth a man child, who was to rule all nations with a rod of iron: and her child was caught up unto God, and to His throne". Revelation 12: 1-6. The only comment I make is to remind you that "the woman [already shown in a previous chapter to represent the true Church] fled into the wilderness, where she hath a place prepared of God, that they should feed her there a thousand two hundred and three score days". Verse 6. Logic, as well as Spirit-inspired revelation, supports the contention that the Church remains on the earth throughout the Great Tribulation.

A brief explanation of the other case of translation shown in The Revelation should suffice. The incident involves the "two witnesses" who "prophesy a thousand two hundred and three score days." This is the duration of the Great Tribulation. "And when they shall have finished their testimony, the beast that ascended out of the bottomless pit shall make war against them, and kill them. . . . And after three days and a half the spirit of life from God entered into them, . . . And they heard a great voice from heaven saying unto them, Come up hither. And they ascended up to heaven in a cloud." Revelation 11: 3, 7, 11, 12.

A number of items appear here. In the first place there is no warrant for supposing these two witnesses represent the whole Church, or any part thereof. Only they are involved. And here take special notice — they are translated to heaven *at the end of the Tribulation.* I cannot refrain from making some observations. In view of the fact that God does allow these two saints to be in the Tribulation; that they are permitted to be persecuted by the Antichrist and his evil associates, and that unto death; and that they continue upon the earth until the full end of the Great Tribulation, what happens to the objection that God would not allow His beloved saints to go through the Tribulation, and to face its trials. He will permit this to happen to these two choice men of God. Why am I to expect favors bestowed upon me not granted to such giants of Godliness? To claim such favoritism for myself would be sheer presumption; indeed, even impudence — don't you agree?

The Rapture, because taught in Scripture, *is* important, but it should be regarded as God treats it—as only *relatively* important. It is merely an adjunct with not more than casual meaning. *The Rapture of the Church is implied in The Revelation; but a Pre-tribulation-rapture is not found there.* It requires a vivid imagination and skilful manipulation of Scripture to invent a Pre-tribulation-rapture. I was about to say it takes wilful determination to "read in", and dishonest interpretation to bring out, what is not therein. Many absurd and unwarranted twists are given to otherwise simple, plain, straightforward statements in The Revelation.

Many times have I read, or heard, the statement: "The Church is not seen after chapter four, verse one". Whoever says that is either dishonest with the truth, or woefully ignorant of the facts. It is quite true that the word "Church" is not found following chapter four, verse one. Indeed, the word "Church" is not used at all in The Revelation. The word "church" is used speaking of local congregations, and meeting-houses. In fact "churches" is the last word of chapter three. The "churches" are organizations; but "Church" with its larger and truer meaning of being an "organism" or the "body of Christ", is nowhere employed. However, other terms used throughout the Bible to designate the Church are used all through The Revelation — such words as "saint", "elect", "brethren". If these words are to be understood as designating Christians, or the "Church", elsewhere in the Word of God, then there is no logical reason to say they do not mean this, but something else, when used in The Revelation. Only the desire, or the attempt to bolster a false teaching would lead to such a perversion of Scripture.

No Change In The Status Of The Church

I know of no statement in The Revelation that would lead us to suppose there will be any change in the status of the Church when the Tribulation commences. No removal of its presence. No cessation of its function. There will undoubtedly be a curtailment of its activities by being restricted through decrees of Antichrist. The Church will be present to give its witness whenever and wherever possible. As the Tribulation grows in scope and seriousness, the Church will carry on its witnessing. Many will be martyred because they defied the Antichrist and endeavored to preach the truth which will be contrary to his principles. When the fifth of the seven seals are broken, John says: "I saw under the altar the souls of them *that were slain for the Word of God, and for the testimony which they held.* . . . And white robes were given unto every one of them, that they should rest for a little season, until their *fellow servants ALSO and their brethren,* that should be killed as they were, should be fulfilled". Revelation 6: 9, 11. If these are not Christians, and thus members of the Church, why are white robes of divine righteousness given to them? Why refer to them as "fellow servants" and "brethren"? These are names given to Christians.

If the Church will not be present during the Tribulation, and the reign of Antichrist, why should God give the special message from heaven saying that *then* is when the *"saints"* will need endurance, and perseverance, to obey the commandments of God and to keep faith with Jesus and contend for the faith of Christ? Why does He give the comforting beatitude: "Blessed are the dead *which die in the Lord from henceforth*: yea, saith the Spirit, that they may rest from their labours". If the Church has been raptured and removed from the earth then this is all misleading and superfluous. Why, why, I ask, does God do it?

"Blessed Is He That Watcheth"

The foregoing, it seems, furnishes ample proof as it progresses that the Church is in the Tribulation. A striking fact appears in chapter sixteen where the Church is shown to be on earth at the very end of the Tribulation. A study of the many Scriptures telling of the Battle of Armageddon will show that the conflict

is to be brief and bloody. It is not a war but a battle.
No where and in no way is it ever spoken of as a war
— always as a battle. "For I will gather all nations
against Jerusalem to battle." Zechariah 14:2. "To gather them to the battle of that great day of God Almighty." Revelation 16:14. A war is usually a long-
drawn-out conflict made up of a series of engagements
called battles. A battle usually is a brief and a bloody
encounter. This is true of Armageddon. Ample evidence is contained in Scripture to show it will be fought
on the last day of this age. *It is at the time of this
battle that the Lord comes as a thief.* This is "according
to Scriptures" and is not according to man's Pre-tribulation fallacy. Let me give it to you as we have it in
God's own Word: "And I saw three unclean spirits
like frogs come out of the mouth of the dragon, and out
of the mouth of the beast, and out of the mouth of the
false prophet. For they are the spirits of devils, working miracles, which go forth unto the kings of the earth
and of the whole world, to gather them to the battle
of that great day of God Almighty. *Behold, I come as
a thief. Blessed is he that watcheth, and keepeth his
garments* lest he walk naked, and they see his shame.
And he gathered them together into a place called in
the Hebrew tongue Armageddon". Revelation 16:13-16.

There we have the truth. At the time of the Battle
of Armageddon the Lord will come *as a thief;* so He
exhorts His Church to watchfulness. "Watch ye therefore, and pray always, that ye may be accounted
worthy to escape all these things [including the Battle
of Armageddon] that shall come to pass." Luke 21:36.
He even pronounces a beatitude: "Blessed is he that
watcheth and keepeth his garments" unsoiled in this
time of great and widespread evil and idolatry. Only
the Church could properly be given such an exhortation

and warning. The wicked have no garments of righteousness to "keep unspotted".

The least we can say here is, that if the Church has been raptured, then this is absurd and superfluous. God might just as well have saved His breath. It is wasted effort; and who is to say what else is superfluous in Scripture teaching? At least, one should admit we may have a case here. Some may even be led to abandon such an unscriptural theory as Pre-tribulation-rapturism.

CHAPTER SEVENTEEN

"Full Of Holes"

Pre-tribulation-rapturism is a modern ism. It is a "strong delusion". Satan has foisted it upon the Church in these last days. It is evidently a diabolical delusion deliberately designed by the devil to deceive unwary Christians, "that they should believe a lie". 2 Thessalonians 2:11. Strong words — you say. A serious charge! Yes, but made with Scripture proof to back it. The fallacy is shot full of holes — large holes. It can't hold water.

It is said that the Church will be raptured before the coming of the Antichrist and the beginning of the Great Tribulation because Paul so teaches in 2 Thessalonians 2:7. Said he: "For the mystery of iniquity doth already work: only he who now letteth [hindereth] will let [hinder], until he be taken out of the way". Here the apostle tells of the restraining forces that will hinder the coming of the full flood of final wickedness and terrors of the Tribulation brought on by "that man of sin . . . the son of perdition", the Antichrist. It is assumed, and so taught by Pre-tribulation-rapturists, that the one who hinders is the Holy Spirit. So, the contention is, the Holy Spirit will leave the world, and return to heaven, taking the Church with Him, thus removing the barrier that held back the manifestation of the Antichrist and the deluge of sin and sorrow and suffering of the Tribulation period.

This interpretation of Paul's statement also is full of holes. It is known that the words of verse six "ye know what withholdeth" literally mean "that which restrains". But it is false to teach that "taken out of the way" means "taken out of the world". Paul reminds the saints that they knew the identity of the one who is to restrain, for he wrote: "And now ye know what withholdeth". Verse 6. The source of their knowledge may have been two-fold. We may assume that the faithful apostle had told them: for in verse five he says: "Remember ye not, that when I was yet with you, I told you these things?". But Paul knew what the Scripture teaches in Genesis six, concerning the days of Noah. Before the deluge came, opportunity was given the antediluvians to repent and turn to God. However, the time was limited and a deadline was set by God Himself. The time-limit was clearly set down as the ultimatum was delivered: "yet his days shall be an hundred and twenty years". The flood stands as a type of the Day of the Lord which comes "immediately after the tribulation". Before the flood could come and the age end, the Spirit must cease to "strive with man". The Spirit would restrain up to a certain point, beyond that He would no longer "strive with man". At the time set, the restraining ceased and the flood came. The Holy Spirit was the Restrainer then, He is the Restrainer now, and will continue in this capacity until a point to be reached in the last days of this age. However, it is important to remember that the Spirit did not depart from the world, but remained with Noah as he "walked with God" on the earth, and so enabled him to "endure unto the end" of the age; and then he entered into the ark when the flood came to destroy the wicked.

It has been the teaching of some scholars that "that which restraineth" is the power of Christian ethics and truths held by Christian nations. This is said to act as a restraining influence upon a world inclined to Godlessness and lawlessness. And these scholars have something in this teaching.

One of the earlier and popular interpretations of the "one that restraineth" is that Paul had in mind the Holy Roman Empire. Perhaps it is true Paul hesitated to set down in words what he meant (which would not have been the case if he meant the Holy Spirit) because he had in mind the Roman Empire. The impersonal influence was the magnificent system of law and justice throughout the Roman world. Chrysostom, one of the earliest and most able of the Church Fathers wrote: "But speaking here of the Roman empire, he does so, and with good reason, enigmatically and obscurely. For he had no wish to provoke needless hostility or to incur superfluous risk". Whether correct, or not, these views show there are other interpretations — and good ones.

The preponderance of evidence found in the text we are considering and its context and also in the Noah type, proves, to my mind, that the restraining force is the Holy Spirit, and was so regarded by Paul. However, whatever it is that restrains, Paul merely states that it is to "be taken out of the way". Are we justified in saying, dogmatically, that "out of the way" means "out of the world"? No. I readily admit it means the restraining influence will cease to restrain because it is "taken out of the way". But I do not admit that it will be taken out of the world. This would be unnecessary in order to restrain. If it is the Holy Spirit, then all He would need to do to permit the advent of "that lawless one" and the inrush of "lawlessness" would be to "step aside" or "be taken out of the way" — not removed to heaven, or any place out of the earth. If He were removed to heaven, then who would carry on the work of conviction and regeneration of sinners during the Tribulation? If His presence was needed to do this at the opening of this age, then it will be needed also at the close of it. You see what I mean when I say the popular view is full of holes.

CHAPTER EIGHTEEN

"The Day Of Martyrs"

Pre-tribulation-rapturism has become, to many, a grand obsession. It seems to represent "heaven's magnificent extra". They make the Rapture of the Church the ultimate of Christian experience in this age. To them it is the beckoning horizon on this pilgrim journey — the goal to achieve. Talk about the Rapture rolls off their tongues as a pleasant platitude. With many it is the sweetest morsel in the whole feast of Gospel truth.

The whole Pre-tribulation-rapture structure is weak. It is doomed to fall of its own weight because built upon forced and false interpretations of Scripture and the sands of sophistry. It can't stand. It is cracking now. The crash is inevitable — "and great was [will be] the fall thereof".

Someone has written, erroneously of course: "For us there shall be no experience with the coming actors, nor with the clash and crash of nations. Deliverance is promised". Yes, deliverance is assured — as Daniel, the three Hebrew children and others, have known it: "and others were tortured, not accepting deliverance [by removal]; that they might obtain a better resurrection". Hebrews 11:35. God could have kept Daniel out of the lions' den, and the three Hebrew children out of the furnace, but it was His glory to preserve them in it.

A New Era of Persecution

It is human nature to think that God is good only when He makes us comfortable. Christianity is a religion of comfort; but not a comfortable religion. Many have said to me: "Why, God would not let His people go into the Great Tribulation and suffer". By raising this objection, they thought they had given an unanswerable argument in favor of Pre-tribulation-rapturism. This statement, of course, is so absurd and untrue, one is amazed it should be offered. Past history and present-day events brand it as being false and foolish. It flies into the face of facts. There have been many instances of organized opposition to Christians and persecution of the Church. Our Lord faithfully taught this would be the case. "In the world ye shall have tribulation"; "and ye shall have tribulation"; "Then shall they deliver you up to be afflicted, and shall kill you; and ye shall be hated of all nations for My name's sake". John 16: 33; Revelation 2: 10; Matthew 24: 9.

Persecution has never been a deterrent to the Church's growth. "The blood of martyrs is the seed of the Church." Christians have thrived upon it. When, I ask you, did God ever favor His saints by removing them from the place of persecution? the answer is: At no time.

"The days of the martyrs", which is a familiar phrase with Church historians, have been many and frequent. These words are taking on a new and dreadful significance again, for the Church is plunging headlong into a new era of persecution. *God will let His people face tribulation, because He always has.* Can anyone say that uncounted numbers have not already faced conditions comparable, in some respects, to the days of the Great Tribulation? The Tribulation will be the "Great Tribulation" in the sense of scope and seriousness; but so far as human suffering or torture is concerned, it is doubtful if any new means of diabolical torture could be devised. After all, one can suffer only so much physical agony and mental anguish. There are only so many ways to inflict suffering; just a limited number of ways to face death. No doubt these have already been exploited. Perhaps millions have experienced suffering and death through them, and others will. To say that God is too good to let His children go into the Tribulation is absurd. If it is true, then I confess I fail to understand the reason why He permitted such a record as I find in Hebrews 11:32-38: "And what shall I more say? for time would fail me to tell . . . of the prophets who . . . stopped the mouths of lions, quenched the violence of fire, escaped the edge of the sword, out of weakness were made strong, waxed valiant in fight, turned to flight the armies of the aliens. . . . Others were tortured, . . . and others had trial of cruel mockings and scourgings, yea, moreover of bonds and imprisonment: they were stoned, they were sawn asunder, were tempted, were slain with the sword: they wandered about in sheepskins and goatskins; being destitute, afflicted, tormented; . . . they wandered in deserts and mountains, and in dens and caves of the earth". Consider the various forms of torture inflicted and the many methods used to cause death here in this shocking narrative, then remember that the only method used to put Tribulation martyrs to death, according to the record, is beheading. John says: "I saw the souls of them that were beheaded for the witness of Jesus". Revelation 20:4.

I had preached on "The Atomic Age and the End of the Age". A Christian came and anxiously inquired: "What about the saints who perished in Hiroshima? I have always been led to believe such things would not occur while the Church was on earth". My answer was: "I can answer the question to your satisfaction only if you are willing to rethink what has been taught about the time of the rapture". You see, it would be difficult today to prove to multitudes of faithful Christians in various places in the world that we are not already facing Great Tribulation. We are not in the Great Tribulation of the end of the age, but there are many in other nations who would quickly inform you *they are facing tribulation.* For them it is as dreadful as any tribulation could possibly be. Jesus said there was to be a "beginning of sorrows", Matthew 24: 8; followed closely by the "great tribulation". Verse 21. Evidently both world and church are passing through that "beginning of sorrows" now, and so are rapidly approaching the Great Tribulation.

I was in Saskatoon, Saskatchewan, conducting a Bible conference a few weeks ago. While there, a field representative of the Council of Christian Leadership, addressing a gathering of Christians said: "Never in the history of the world have so many been tortured and enslaved as now. . . . Religious persecution has assumed hideous proportions. . . . One Colombian pastor who saw me only two days before I left the country was taken by the police and bandits and cut to pieces. A piece of his body was sent to each member of his flock. . . . In two Colombian cities all Protestants were driven out".

The Home Director for Great Britain of the China Inland Mission and Chairman of the English Keswick has written: "The problem of the Christian and persecution is at our doors. It is already a living issue (or a dying one!) in half of Europe and in half of Asia. In certain European countries a decision to worship only the Lord God as Scripture and conscience dictate, has already proved a matter of life and death. . . . Has the Christian in certain countries any guarantee of immunity from the sorrows which the brethren are experiencing in others? We are facing a new challenge, which may be equal to that of Nero and Domitian in the first centuries, or to that of the Inquisition and Marian persecutions of the seventeenth and contiguous centuries".

"A carefully documented release from Washington, D. C., reveals the following atrocities committed by the Roman Catholics in Colombia, South America, against Protestants within the past year: twenty-four chapels burned, five confiscated; eight bombed, dynamited, or otherwise damaged; two closed by force. In each case the congregations have been scattered under threat of death. In some, the local preachers have been murdered, and many of the homes of the Christians burned, and their property stolen." These persecutions, directed against Christians simply because they *are* followers of Christ are by no means confined to any one area, but are rapidly spreading with intensity across the world.

Ponder this dispatch with a Berlin date line: "An all-out offensive will be launched against the 'reactionary' church-leadership in the East German Republic after the October 15 elections. . . . Dr. Steinhoff predicted that 'in half a year there will no longer be any church question'. . . . He said he would enforce 'changes' in church administration which have been recommended by 'progressive clergymen who stand firm behind the government'". Stripped of its verbiage this means simply that the East German Church is expected to be destroyed within six months. What is happening to Christians in many places is summed up, with what may be called humor, by some Chinese believers.

"First," they say, "they nod their heads at us. Then they shake their heads at us. Then they cut our heads off". Truly Tribulation conditions are beginning to develop. This anyone can see.

CHAPTER NINETEEN

"Sound the Trumpet"

Perhaps the most significant "signs of the times" are the religious signs. They are two-fold. 1) The sign of great spiritual apostasy — "a falling away" from the faith. 2) The sign of great spiritual apathy. Jesus predicted this, when in Matthew 24:12, He said: "And because iniquity shall abound, the love of many shall wax cold". We are plunging into this period of apathy and dearth. Surely this was in the mind of Daniel when he predicted, "And he [Antichrist] shall speak great words against the Most high, and shall wear out the saints of the Most high". Daniel 7:25.

Already there is a sad lament among the faithful over the paralyzing apathy that is settling like a dread miasma upon the people of God and the churches. Many are asking the reason for it. Everywhere I go, I find noble and sincere pastors, who are heart-broken over the condition. There are no doubt a number of conditions responsible for this spiritual declension. Without any question, it is, among other things, the logical result of the deadening effect of the flesh-pleasing doctrine of Pre-tribulation-rapturism. Think this over! Many souls have been lulled to sleep by the soothing influence of this fallacy. If the Church is to be raptured before the Tribulation, then why develop faith and be on fire with a blazing, all-out devotion to Christ? Just sit still; fold your arms; rock yourself to sleep. The voice of the archangel, the trumpet of God will awaken you at the descent of Christ. You won't need great faith, or deep devotion to remain true to Christ in the time when the Antichrist reigns, because you will be raptured before he takes over. This is the general attitude. The result is, many are dozing.

Everywhere the enquiry is being made: What is to be the next thing in evangelism? What new movement can we inaugurate to awaken sleeping saints, and arouse drowsy Christians? One answer is: Destroy the sleep-producing fallacy of Pre-tribulation-rapturism by sounding the trumpet of Bible truth! "Therefore be ye also ready: for in such an hour as ye think not the Son of man cometh." Matthew 24:44.